Treasures On Your Doorstep

National
Park Service
Centennial
Edition
1916-2016

Buy further copies of this book at:
www.createspace.com/3861485
Treasuresonyourdoorstep.com
Or Amazon.com and other retailers

Find the Treasures On Your Doorstep blog at:
http://treasuresonyourdoorstep.blogspot.com/

Front cover photograph by Julia Lynam:
*Pedestals at White Sands National Monument in New Mexico are
formed when sand consolidated by plants growing up through high
dunes remains trapped after the loose sand of the dune is blown away
by persistent winds.*

ISBN: 0984780513

Treasures On Your Doorstep

∾

The Other National Parks of the USA

by
Julia Lynam

National Park Service Centennial Edition
Celebrating 100 years: 1916-2016

Illustrated by Melanie Gillman and Jessica Valin

Contents

The 400-plus National Park Service units embrace a vast range of habitats and preserve an endless treasure trove of stories. They rightly lay claim to the title of "The Nation's Storyteller". They elicit a huge variety of responses from the human psyche, heart, and soul. Somewhere among the 400 is one, or maybe several, sights and stories that will strike a chord with you, that will pique your interest, that will pull at your heartstrings, that will help your spirit soar.

INTRODUCTION: Read this, please!

Why I wrote this book

Welcome to a new and different way of looking at the treasures that make up the National Park Service of the USA. I've visited and worked in many different National Park properties, or units, and in doing so, I've realized that lots of people in the USA are surprised and delighted to discover the treasures that lie at our very doorsteps.

This book is full of information that I've found myself sharing over and over again with friends and with visitors to these wonderful places. It's information that the rangers would like you to have. It's information that I want everybody to have, because it will unlock so much delight and discovery for you – at such little expense!

What this book is

This is an ideas book. It's intended to get your cranial juices activated: to fire up your imagination, open up your visionary capacity, and get you moving. If you already visit as many National Park Service (NPS) units as you can in any given year, well, maybe there will be some new ideas here for you, and this book will reinforce and affirm what you're already doing.

If you don't already visit NPS units, you have a treat in store. This book will reveal a fresh prospect: it will be full of exciting suggestions for you and, wow, there are some wonderful discoveries ahead!

Most of the National Park units featured in this book are the less well known ones; the ones that are not actually called "National Parks" but maybe "National Historical Parks" or "National Monuments" or one of many other designations. That's why I've called them "the other National Parks of the USA". If I do sometimes mention an actual "National Park" it's because that one best illustrates a particular point!

Please note that the details in this book are correct at time of publication, February 2016.

Entrance fees, pass prices, numbers of units, their designations and other details may change from time to time. Check before you go.

The scope of this book

The National Park Service has responsibility for some of the federally protected lands of the USA. The National Forest Service, the Bureau of Land Management, the Bureau of Reclamation and the Army Corps of Engineers are among the other bodies looking after other sections of federal land, including certain National Monuments. In some instances, the different organizations cooperate with one another and share administration of certain sites.

The National Park Service is also responsible for maintaining and expanding the National Register of Historic Places, many of which are not in NPS units.

In this book, we're considering "only" the 400-plus sites that the National Park Service itself lists as legally coming under its administration. The nuances can be confusing, but there's no need for that to affect our enjoyment of these natural, historic and cultural treasures.

What this book is not

"Treasures On Your Doorstep" is *not* a travel guide to the NPS units of the United States – there are guidebooks doing that already, and the very best source is the NPS's own elaborate network of web pages, *www.nps.gov*, which are an absolute mine of information that could keep you busy for years. See Chapter 2 for more about this!

So, please get out there and enjoy – walk in the halls of history, feel the breeze in your hair, inhale the scent of spring azalea in the woods, hear the resounding crash of falling water, experience the wonder of the wilderness, the thrill of meeting historical characters or the challenge of piecing together some of the puzzles and mysteries of the past – discover the Treasures On Your Doorstep!

This book is not in any way sponsored or supported by the National Park Service: it has emerged out of my own research and my own experiences in National Park properties.

Julia Lynam,
Burlington, Vermont
February 2016

CHAPTER 1: What and Where

The term "National Park" may conjure up wide vistas of huge mountains, expansive plains, open desert, deep forest, herds of bison, packs of wolves and perhaps schools of manatee. Yes, the National Park Service is about those incomparable places and animals, and yes, go out and enjoy them as often as you can, taking your loved ones with you. And, the National Park system is also much, much more than that: it encompasses many different and fascinating sites; most of them with names other than "National Park".

There's at least one National Park Service (NPS) unit in every one of the 50 states, and the list continues to grow. New properties are added under nearly every Presidential administration. Castle Mountains National Monument, for instance, was designated by President Obama in February 2016. A 21,000-acre stretch of desert embraced by the Mojave National Preserve in southern California, this new NPS unit contains fine examples of Joshua Trees and native desert grassland as well as important archeological sites.

Other recently designated NPS units include:

What's in a name?

Funny, I thought the Delaware Water Gap National Recreation Area would be in Delaware, but it's not: it's in New Jersey and Pennsylvania. Just goes to show that you don't necessarily know about something because you know its name! The same common name may be used in different places for different plants and animals. Early European settlers often named local wildlife after something back home that looked similar – so we ended up with a bird called a "robin" in North America which is very different from the bird called a "robin" in Europe. Even more confusingly, a wildflower may have different common names in different parts of the country and the same common name, like "bluebell", may be used for several different wildflowers! ✿

- Waco Mammoth National Monument in Waco, Texas, where you can view a fossilized herd of Ice Age Columbian mammoths 67,000 years old.
- The three-site Manhattan Project National Historical Park, with locations in New Mexico, Washington and Tennessee, which tells the story of the people, science and engineering that led to the development of the atomic bomb;
- Honoliuli National Monument, Hawaii, the site of a World War II prisoner of war and internment camp;
- Pullman National Monument in Chicago, which tells the story of a utopian workers' community, a unique experiment in social control and the ensuing strike of 1894;
- Harriet Tubman Underground Railroad National Monument in Cambridge, Maryland, which commemorates the life of a fearless woman who helped many black slaves escape to freedom in the North and to eventual emancipation
- Charles Young Buffalo Soldiers National Monument in Xenia, Ohio, which tells the story of a distinguished African American soldier, the first to reach the rank of Colonel in the United States Army, and also, incidentally, the first African American National Park Superintendent;
- Tule Springs Fossil Beds National Monument near Las Vegas, Nevada, another Ice Age site, which is home to the rare Las Vegas bearpoppy as well as fossilized bones of extinct horses, camels, bison and the dire wolf;
- The Flight 93 National Memorial in southwestern Pennsylvania, which was dedicated in September 2011 to commemorate some very recent history, the tragic events of September 11, 2001.

Designations are some-
times changed: in January
2013, Pinnacles National
Monument, a home of the
California condor, became
Pinnacles National Park. It
took an act of Congress to
move Pinnacles to this very
high level of recognition and
protection.

Give them Time!

It takes a while for new
National Park units to
get up and running, so
some recently designated
ones may not yet have
Visitor Centers and other
facilities. ᴈ

As well as in all the states, there are National Park prop-
erties in the District of Columbia, American Samoa, Guam,
Puerto Rico, and the US Virgin Islands. They're all listed in
Appendix 2 of this book.

On Your Doorstep

If you're just starting out on an exploration of NPS units,
how about taking a first step by getting to know those in
your own state?

The National Park Service's own web site is a very good
place for this. Go to *http://www.nps.gov* and use the "Find a
Park" tool at the top right hand side of the home page.

The extent of your first step in discovering the treasures
on your doorstep varies depending on where you live: if
you're in Connecticut, Illinois, Vermont or Rhode Island, you

have only one or two sites to visit, so get going to Weir Farm National Historic Site, Lincoln Home National Historic Site or Roger Williams National Memorial. They're all quite small.

If, on the other hand, you live in California, you have currently 28 NPS units, ranging from places like the 760,000 acre Yosemite National Park, which was, incidentally the first area set aside by the Federal Government to be preserved for its scenic beauty (that was in 1864 – it wasn't called a national park until 1890) to the Eugene O'Neill National Historic Site in Danville, where reservations are required if you want to visit the former home of the USA's only Nobel Prize-winning playwright.

California has some very large parks (of course!), including the largest in the lower 48, Death Valley National Park, which encompasses over three million acres, stretches 140 miles from north to south, and ranges in elevation from minus

Home Comfort

Abraham Lincoln's comfortable home in Springfield, Illinois has been restored to its appearance in the year 1860. Admission is free but tickets are limited, so get there early! It's quite a contrast to his birthplace in Hodgenville, Kentucky, another NPS site, where a symbolic wooden cabin stands within a memorial building. Lincoln's boyhood home in Lincoln City, Indiana is also an NPS unit. ✑

282 feet in the Badwater Basin to 11,049 feet on Telescope Peak: you can stand in the one and look up at the other!

California also has a lot of smaller units like the Devil's Postpile National Monument in the Sierra Nevada, which cares for a beautiful 101-foot waterfall as well as one of the world's finest examples of columnar basalt. That's volcanic lava cooled and solidified into huge hexagonal columns – cool is the word for it!

In Virginia, thanks largely to the tragic war that embroiled the country in conflict from 1861 to 1865, you'll also have your work cut out visiting all the NPS sites. They're not all battlefields, though: there are some fascinating historic places like the Maggie L. Walker National Historic Site that celebrates the life and achievement of the first black woman to run a bank in the USA.

In the District of Columbia, there are many and varied NPS sites, ranging from the White House and the Lincoln Memorial to the green oasis of Rock Creek Park, which offers beautiful natural scenery, a rich cultural heritage and the only planetarium in the NPS!

Large and Small

The smallest unit in the NPS system is the Thaddeus Kosciusko National Memorial in Philadelphia, a former boarding house where a Polish freedom fighter who had joined in with the American Revolutionary War languished for ten months in the 1790s. He received many visitors, including Thomas Jefferson who said that Kosciusko was "as pure a son of liberty as I have ever known".

The largest unit in the whole system is Wrangell-St. Elias National Park in Alaska with 8,323,148 acres (13,004.9 square miles). It's usually paired with the contiguous Wrangell-St. Elias National Preserve which has 4,852,753 acres (7,582.4 square miles) for a total of more than 13 million acres of Alaskan wilderness on a grand scale, 25 percent of it covered by glaciers – at time of writing.

In between these extremes you have, among others, such hidden treasures as Montezuma Castle National Monument in Arizona with its deep turquoise pool and ancient cliff dwellings, clues to a lost culture; the vast ocean of solidified lava at Craters of the Moon National Monument and Preserve in Idaho; the celebrated Mount Rushmore National Memorial in South Dakota with its controversial cliff carvings; the spectacular Lake Superior shoreline at Pictured Rocks National Lakeshore in Michigan's Upper Peninsula and Nicodemus National Historic Site in Kansas, an historic all-black town established during the Reconstruction period.

All the People

National Park units represent the history of all the people of the United States. They don't shy away from the truth. The internment camp for Japanese Americans at Manzanar in California is a National Historic Site; Washita Battlefield National Historic Site in Cheyenne, Oklahoma protects and interprets the place where the village of Peace Chief Black Kettle was attacked by the US Cavalry led by Lt. Col. George A. Custer in November 1868.

All the terrestrial units, of course, stand on ground once occupied by indigenous people, and many of them acknowledge this and include the history of their original inhabitants in their interpretive and educational efforts. Some units specifically preserve the history of American Indian people past and present. Among these are Canyon de Chelly National Monument in the Navajo territory of Arizona, and Mesa Verde National Park in Colorado, which preserves ancient cliff dwellings, as does Gila Cliff Dwellings National Monument in New Mexico.

Ocmulgee National Monument in Georgia honors 17,000 years of continuous human habitation, interpreting the history of the Mississippian culture, while Hopewell Culture National Historical Park in Ohio protects earthworks dating from more than 2000 years ago.

"There stands Jackson like a stone wall" statue of General
"Stonewall" Jackson at Manassas National Battlefield Park, Virginia

The stunning ruins at Chaco Culture National Historical Park in New Mexico, designated by the United Nations as a World Heritage Site because of their special importance to the common heritage of humanity, are an incredible record of a mysterious and advanced civilization now lost to us.

African American Heritage

The NPS tries to make things easy for those of you who have a particular interest – for instance, to find out more about units that focus particularly on African American heritage, go to *nps.gov/history/aahistory*. There, you can access a list of more than 25 African American Experience Parks which include such places as the George Washington Carver National Monument in Diamond, Missouri; the Tuskegee Institute National Historic Site in Alabama and the Little Rock Central High School National Historic Site in Little Rock, Arkansas.

Latino Heritage

The specifically Latino heritage of the USA is traced in such units as Cabrillo National Monument in San Diego, California; the Castillo de San Marcos National Monument in St. Augustine, Florida; Chamizal National Memorial in El Paso, Texas and El Morro National Monument in Ramah, New Mexico, where travelers throughout the ages, including Spanish conquistadors, left inscriptions carved in the rock – their graffiti are our historic treasures!

San Juan National Historic Site in Old San Juan, Puerto Rico, preserves fortifications dating from the 16th century and recalling the long struggle of the European powers to establish supremacy in the Caribbean.

Many other sites relevant to the American Latino experience are identified on the NPS web page, and you can find a list of them by searching for *American Latino Heritage*. The list also includes many sites on the National Register of Historic Places which are not, strictly speaking, part of the NPS.

They're nearer than you think!

If there's an NPS site in every state, then there's likely to be one or more near you! You may not be able to pop over to San Juan, or to Kalaupapa National Historical Park on the Hawaiian island of Molokai for a Sunday afternoon picnic, but if you happen to live in or near southern New Hampshire, for instance, you might easily take a run up to Cornish to visit the elegant St. Gaudens (pronounced God-ens) National Historic Site and maybe enjoy a Sunday afternoon concert.

If you live in or near St. Louis, Missouri, then you have the Jefferson National Expansion Memorial, better known as the Gateway Arch, within striking distance. Here you can ride up in an elevator to the top of the sweeping arch – claustrophobics may wish to proceed with caution! If you live in the city of Los Angeles, you have the Santa Monica Mountains National

Recreation Area within a short drive. Made up of a number of different sites, this unit has the dubious distinction of being partly in the 90210 Beverly Hills zip code area!

Tripping Through History

Simply reading the list of names of NPS units is like a trip through the history, culture, and

> **Native Plants**
>
> Kalaupapa National Historical Park tells the story of the enforced isolation of people suffering from Hansen's disease (leprosy) between 1866 and 1969. Because of its remote location, this NPS unit is one of few places in the Hawaiian Islands that retain areas where plants native to the islands still grow. ✑

ecology of this nation! They're in our wild and open areas, and they're in and around our cities. Here are some of the urban units: the descriptions in quotes come from the NPS itself.

NEW YORK CITY

- African Burial Ground National Monument "A Sacred Space in Manhattan"
- Castle Clinton National Monument "Built to Keep Millions Out..."
- Federal Hall National Memorial "Birthplace of American Government"
- Gateway National Recreation Area "A Park that's more than the sum of its parts..."

- General Grant National Memorial "Let Us have Peace"
- Governors Island National Monument "A Silent Sentinel in New York Harbor"
- Sagamore Hill National Historic Site, Theodore Roosevelt's Home;
- Saint Paul's Church National Historic Site "Living History in a Cemetery?"
- Statue of Liberty National Monument "Liberty Enlightening the World"
- Theodore Roosevelt Birthplace National Historic Site "The Childhood of a Renowned President".

SAN FRANCISCO

- Eugene O'Neill National Historic Site "O'Neill in California"
- Fort Point National Historic Site "Civil War Living History"
- John Muir National Historic Site "Father of the National Park Service"
- Golden Gate National Recreation Area "Parks for the People." Has many constituent units including the Presidio and Muir Woods National Monument;
- San Francisco Maritime National Historical Park "Where Your Imagination Can Travel to the 19th Century".

BOSTON AREA

- Adams National Historical Park "Oh my sweet little farm"
- Boston African American National Historic Site "Freedom is a constant struggle."

- Boston Harbor Islands National Recreation Area "Minutes Away: Worlds Apart"
- Boston National Historical Park "The revolution was in the minds and hearts of the People."
- Frederick Law Olmsted National Historic Site "Designing an American Landscape"
- John Fitzgerald Kennedy National Historic Site "Many Happy Memories"
- Longfellow House-Washington's Headquarters National Historic Site "Where American Character and Culture were shaped."
- Minute Man National Historical Park "A Revolution Begins – a Nation is Born"
- Salem Maritime National Historic Site "To the Farthest Ports of the Rich East"
- Saugus Iron Works National Historic Site "Explore the birthplace of the American iron and steel industry."

There they are, sprinkled across the country from your doorstep to the wild blue yonder. Take the subway, walk, cycle, or hit the open road; even fly. NPS units eagerly await you.

Units range from the urban, like Rock Creek Park, easily accessible to city dwellers in the nation's capital, to the unthinkably remote, like the country's largest unaltered river basin and watershed, in the Noatak National Preserve in Alaska. With no road leading there and no developed facilities, a visit to Noatak is an adventure indeed! The number of visitors to Noatak in 2014 is not available – there may have been none. In that same year the remote Aniakchak National Monument and Preserve in Alaska, home to the six-mile wide, 2,500-foot-deep remains of a volcano, welcomed 134 people! Compare that to the nearly 14 million who visited the Blue Ridge Parkway (in North Carolina and Virginia) in 2014. Aniakchak rather coyly advertises: "No lines, no waiting"!

One of the most surprising sights I've seen in a National Park unit is kids happily sledding in June, with the temperature in the 90s! Where can you do this? White Sands National Monument in southern New Mexico, where the open dunes are like snow – and the local people know it! Many schools and families from El Paso, Las Cruces, and Alamogordo head out for a day's sledding and picnicking to celebrate the end of the school year. They're using their local unit – are you using yours?

Accessibility for People with Handicaps

Many NPS units have specifically handicap-accessible features like the desert boardwalk at the aforementioned White Sands National Monument or a tactile map at Hopewell Culture NHP. Visitor Centers and other modern buildings are mandated to be accessible, although this can sometimes present challenges with historical structures.

For example, Scotty's Castle in Death Valley National Park was built in the 1920s by a man, Albert Johnson, who had his own severe mobility issues, but the Castle gained a chairlift to the second floor only after it became part of a National Park (check that the chairlift's working before you go there!).

Wheelchairs are often available for use at historic houses and other sites, so that you don't have to remain standing - or sit on the antique furniture - while the ranger's talking. It's wise to ask about accessibility beforehand so you can plan your visit carefully.

If you're a US citizen with a permanent disability, you can get a special "Access" pass giving you free entry to NPS units. More about this in Chapter 4 "The Best Bargains".

∾

CHAPTER 2: Finding Your Way

Back at home, sitting with your trusty computer, you can explore all these places through the NPS web site at *http://www.nps.gov* – the *.gov* bit is really, really important because commercial and other web pages sometimes mimic the official ones, so you want to be sure you're in the right place. If you find a web page for a particular park unit, make sure it's the official one with the suffix *.gov*. Information posted on non-official sites may be outdated or inaccurate.

The National Park Foundation, which is the official charitable partner of the NPS and supports many great programs, also has a very informative web site at *nationalparks.org*.

On the *nps.gov* home page you can search the entire list of 400-plus NPS properties – they call them "units" so I'll call them that, too. In a minute I'll explain why we have to use that term if we want to be clear, rather than just saying "parks".

To pinpoint a specific unit, you can search the list by state on *nps.gov*, look at the alphabetical list at *nationalparks.org*. If you know the name of the one you want to check out, there's a really fun way of finding its own web page by making a guess at what the nickname - the code - is for each unit.

Use or Lose!

If you don't have Internet access at home, or while you're traveling, there's another oft-forgotten public facility that offers free Internet access, and that's the public library! Use them or lose them! Check opening hours! ☜

Check your url!

Reminder: make sure you're consulting the official National Park website for the unit you're researching! If it's not *nps.gov*, it may not offer accurate information. ☜

The Code

The code is used throughout the National Park Service as a shorthand way of referring to a unit. It's usually made up of the first two letters of the first two words of the unit's name. So, Grant-Kohrs Ranch National Historic Site in Montana, for instance, is GRKO, Padre Island National Seashore in Texas is PAIS, and Capitol Reef National Park in Utah is, sweetly, CARE - get the idea? If the unit has only one word in its name, then you use the first four letters of that: Alcatraz (part of Golden Gate NRA) is ALCA; Bandelier National Monument in New Mexico is BAND. Two of them have four-letter names, so you use the whole name: Obed Wild and Scenic River in Tennessee is OBED, and Zion National Park, Utah is ZION.

If you want to get to a certain unit's web page quickly, you just type in *nps.gov/noca* or *nps.gov/moru*, and cut out a couple of steps.

This system has some charming anomalies. Carlsbad Caverns National Park, New Mexico, for instance, would be CACA, which is a rude word in Spanish, so they use CAVE instead – neat, eh? And rather than make a JOKE of the 35th President of the US, they very carefully call his birthplace the John *Fitzgerald* Kennedy National Historic Site, NPS code JOFI!

As more units are added, though, the code may become harder to guess: President William Jefferson Clinton Birthplace Home National Historic Site in Hope, Arkansas is "WICL" because the first two letters of the first two words "PRWI" were already taken by Prince William Forest Park in Virginia! Prince William, incidentally, has its own special designation – it's the only "Forest Park" in the whole system, and, confusingly, its name doesn't include the word "National"!

"Park" or "Unit"?

Some people, especially employees of the Service, refer to all NPS properties as "parks". For instance, they'll ask a newly-met colleague: "Which park do you work in?" But this seems to confuse many visitors, so I'm doing something different in this book.

Within the US National Park system, there are, at time of writing, 59 places actually called "*Something* National Park". They tend to be the ones that most people have heard of: Yellowstone, Yosemite, Death Valley, Shenandoah, Everglades, Denali, to name but a few, are "National Parks". In "Treasures On Your Doorstep" we're focusing on the others, the ones with different names, although the odd "National Park" does seem to creep into the book every now and then.

The whole system includes some quite unexpected sites and many different designations, such as:

- National Monuments;
- National Historical Parks;
- National Historic Sites;
- National Recreation Areas;
- National Seashores;
- National Scenic Rivers;
- National Military Parks;
- National Battlefield Parks; and
- National Preserves.

There are more than 20 different designations and more than 400 different units in all. You can find a list of all the current designations in Appendix 1 at the end of this book.

All these units are part of the National Park Service, funded from the Federal budget, donations, fees and endowments, and they all belong to the people of the United States – they are there to be both preserved and enjoyed!

Throughout this book I'm going to refer to them as "units". That tells us that we're talking about a lot more than the 59 or so that are called "National Parks". You'll get used to it.

In most of the units, you'll see employees, including rangers, wearing green and gray uniforms and sporting the arrowhead badge on their shoulders.

More importantly, all these places are dedicated to the mission of the National Park Service, and because part

National Monuments are not large statues!

Weird as it might sound, a National Monument is not a large statue but a type of National Park designated by the President alone rather than by Congress.

We have President Theodore Roosevelt to thank for this strange situation. He established Devil's Tower National Monument in Wyoming, using the Antiquities Act of 1906, which has since been used by many presidents to protect places like the Grand Canyon (1908) and Death Valley (1933).

So a National Monument may be a large park-like area with nary a statue in it.

The rather monumental Statue of Liberty (1933), however, *is* actually a National Monument, which makes perfect sense to me! ✎

of that mission is to provide for your enjoyment, they'll be welcoming places.

Well, that is, the humans, where they're present, will be welcoming: the wildlife may not be so keen to see you (see Chapter 6). I say "where they're present" because some of these units have no designated NPS field staff attached to them, at least, none you're likely to see. The Appalachian National

> **Symbolic Badge**
>
> The National Park Service's arrowhead badge symbolizes the cultural and natural resources entrusted to its care. The elements on the badge have significance: the bison stands for the animals; the sequoia tree and grass for the plants, and the mountains and water for the environment. These individual items are enclosed in a representation of a stone arrowhead, symbolizing the cultural resources of the country. ∽

Scenic Trail which winds its way more than 2100 miles along the wild mountain ridges of 14 eastern states is a case in point.

Mission

There are strict criteria that have to be met before a new NPS site can be designated, but the bottom line is that these are all places that the people of the United States have decided are worth preserving and conserving for their cultural, historical, and natural significance. They are places, large and small, that the people have decided to care for: that's why knowing about them and visiting them can be important to *you*!

The mission of the National Park Service is based on the text of legislation from 1916. It's currently stated as:

"The National Park Service preserves unimpaired the natural and cultural resources and values of the National Park System for the enjoyment, education, and inspiration of this and future generations. The Park Service cooperates with partners to extend the benefits of natural and cultural resource conservation and outdoor recreation throughout this country and the world."

Preserving something unimpaired while helping people to enjoy it is quite difficult. How do you help people enjoy these resources without impairing them – spoiling them - in any way? Setting foot in a wilderness area changes it; creating and using a footpath in the desert changes it; opening the doors of an historic house instead of keeping it hermetically sealed shortens the life of its furniture and paintings.

So it's not entirely possible both to conserve and to use, and the NPS walks a fine line, always trying to balance the options of conservation and wise use. If you keep that in mind as you read this book and as you enjoy the units you choose to visit, you'll deepen your understanding and appreciation of your National Park units, and perhaps feel moved to do your bit to help preserve and care for them.

Economic Effects

National Park units are not, however, just about preservation, learning and enjoyment. They are also an important, sometimes vital, part of the economy of their local communities and the nation, attracting tourist spending and helping to create jobs.

In its peer-reviewed report "2014 National Park Visitor Spending Effects" the NPS states that its 292.8 million visitors that year spent a total of $15.7 billion in communities within a 60-mile radius of the park, much of it in restaurants, bars, motels and bed and breakfast establishments. This amount of spending, they report, has a knock-on effect in the economy, generating 277,000 jobs nationally and adding $29.7 billion in output to the national economy. Additionally, the NPS itself employs more than 20,000 people.

The NPS reckons that the units return more than $10 to the economy for every $1 the American tax payer invests in them.

So the National Park system adds to the well-being of the nation in many ways and when we visit, we're not just enjoying ourselves and increasing our knowledge, but also participating in the economic prosperity of the nation!

How can you help? Seeking out NPS units, visiting and enjoying is a great start; telling other people about your experiences is a good next step. See chapter 7 for more ideas about participation and support.

❧

CHAPTER 3: Things to Do in NPS Units

Once you've pinpointed your nearest NPS unit, or developed an itinerary of several to visit on your vacation, you can start to discover the stories.

Before you go

Every National Park unit has a tale to tell, a story for you to explore. Some are small, some are large, but they are all part of the natural and cultural history of

Choosing a center

Bill and Myra from Minnesota were visiting a National Historical Park when they explained how they plan their vacations: *"We decide on a part of the country and look for a National Park unit to be the center of our vacation."*

the United States of America - that's why these places have been set aside. They may hold just one story, or many stories: stories of individuals, of tribes, of ethnic or religious minorities; stories of landscapes, natural environments, wild grandeur, historic events, charismatic animals and plants, pivotal inventions and many, many more ingredients of our national heritage.

So you'll get much more out of your visit if you do a little preparation beforehand. We're back to the web site, aren't we: *www.nps.gov*!

If you take some time for research beforehand you'll have an idea of what you want to do at the unit: what area you want to visit, where you want to camp, which building you want to see, even which ranger program you want to join in with. You can also check the likely weather and decide what clothes to wear!

It's a good idea, too, to find out if it's a particularly busy time of year at your chosen unit. Peak season varies around the country, and it can be frustrating to find that all the campsites are already occupied or all the tours fully booked. Think Fall in New England, or New Year in southern California.

If you don't have time to do the research ahead of your visit, take the time when you first arrive to read the brochures, look at the maps, ask some questions. The more you ask, the more you find out: the more you look, the more you see! Many units have complex stories that unfold as you take the time to explore.

When you arrive

What do you do once you get there? You may, of course, have set out with a specific activity in mind – historic research; rock-climbing; white water rafting; astronomy; wildflower viewing; a pilgrimage to the home of an admired president or a place that inspired a poet or conservationist.

If you don't have plans – here come some ideas. If you do have plans – here are some ideas of *other* things to do! Why not try something new?

People visit NPS units for many different reasons, some of them being:

- to breathe the fresh open air;
- to learn about history;
- to see wildlife;
- to relax;
- to enjoy outdoor pursuits;
- to gather information for school projects;
- to expand their minds, broaden their horizons, and stretch their minds as well as their limbs;
- to have fun!

What's *your* reason for visiting?

Even "no reason" is a reason; "just hanging out" may be exactly what you need to do to balance your busy life.

Picnicking in a woodland clearing surrounded by bright butterflies could be just what you need to help you relax. The dark night skies of many NPS units could be your perfect location for star-gazing. Wandering through shady glades or sunlit meadows could bring peace of mind; focusing on the life of Carl Sandberg or John Muir, Frederick Douglass, Clara Barton or Herbert Hoover could take you away from your own concerns, refresh your mind, and challenge you to think differently.

Hiking

Hiking is probably the classic National Park activity! Picture yourself cresting a ridge just as the sun begins to set in glorious shades of red, the songbirds trill their last chorus, and shy elk or black bears slip away into bushes. You stand there, sipping ice-cold water from your insulated water bottle, and you know perfect happiness. We'll talk about hiking safety in Chapter 6.

Camping

Staying overnight inside a unit is a great way to become immersed in its atmosphere. It's also a popular avenue to discovery. Because of their mission to preserve the natural heritage of the country, camping, both in developed and undeveloped sites, is strictly controlled in National Park units. Arrangements and regulations vary greatly among the units, so check before you go. You can make reservations at many National Park and other federal campgrounds throughout the country on the web site *www.recreation.gov.* Be sure to book well ahead.

Other Outdoor Pursuits

Many other activities, including swimming, cycling, canoeing and kayaking, rock climbing, and horseback riding are available in National Park units - the National Park experience can be a very active one! Participatory activities other than ranger-led programs are often organized by commercial concessions which are permitted to operate within certain units.

Information on all this is available from each unit's web page, or from the unit's Visitor Center. Whatever you choose to do, please do it safely.

Dogs: Check Ahead!

There may or may not be a place for your dog – or other pet – in the National Park property you're planning to visit.

Some units with trails welcome dogs, always held on a short leash and under control, of course.

Dogs are not, however, usually allowed in Visitor Centers or in historic buildings or on many sites of historic interest. Nor can they usually be taken on ranger programs or to evening campfire programs. Imagine how many dogs would turn up at these events if they were allowed! And many dogs together usually add up to trouble!

Hiking trails, and the backcountry, too, are often reserved for use by wild animals and people, not dogs. The expanses of open country or wilderness preserved by the National Park Service are intended to give the indigenous wildlife a chance to live unmolested in their natural environment. The domestic dog isn't part of the native wildlife of this country, it's an alien species. And it is by nature a predator. That's why many park units do not allow dogs, even leashed, on their hiking trails. The presence of so many predatory animals would alarm and scare away the native wildlife.

So please check ahead if you're planning to take your pet with you to a National Park unit. You're likely to find that the presence of a dog severely limits where you can go and what you can do. Service animals of course, march to a different drum.

Hunting

About 70 units of the National Park system allow controlled hunting. In order for this to happen, hunting must be specifically permitted by the "enabling" legislation that originally established the unit. Many, but not all, of the units that permit hunting are designated "preserve" or "national recreation area".

Where hunting is allowed, it's governed by state and local regulations and sometimes by additional NPS regulations controlling when and where and how hunting takes place, what weapons are permitted, and how many animals or birds may be killed. It's the hunter's responsibility, as it would be in any other hunting location, to know and abide by these regulations.

Fishing

Many National Park units offer fishing opportunities. State and local regulations apply, with possible additional NPS regulations – just check them, then head out and enjoy yourselves.

Digging Deeper

The NPS experience is likely to be a stimulating, rewarding and even provocative one. You'll learn something about the natural and cultural history of each unit by engaging in any of the activities mentioned above and by reading the brochures and informational signs; but if you want to dig a bit deeper and develop a better understanding of the place, you could try attending a ranger program.

Ranger Programs

At times we may wish to enjoy and commune with nature alone, without someone suggesting ideas to us, and there's plenty of space for that in the National Park units. There is, however, also a place for sensitive and informative "interpretation" that brings us into a better understanding of and empathy with the spirit of the place.

There's a place for the information-hungry to get to grips with details, and there's a place for being able to ask questions and exchange ideas with other visitors. That's where ranger programs come in.

Ranger programs encompass a huge variety of subjects and approaches. Rangers aren't usually given a set script and sent out to parrot it. They're often given a framework and immense creative freedom to fill in that framework in ways that help visitors make intellectual and emotional connections to the scenery, wildlife, history, and significance of the unit.

"I never knew what I was missing. I saw groups of people with rangers and I always thought that was for people who didn't know anything and couldn't do anything on their own, not for me. I went on hiking or biking or exploring by myself. I had no idea what the ranger programs had to offer."

Wendy, Shelburne, Vermont, on attending her first ranger program. ⤴

Most rangers are in the job because they love it. They love the place, the nature, the history, and they think the visitors are pretty neat too. I mean, they have to enjoy talking with lots of different people, don't they? Otherwise they'd be jumping off those beautiful cliffs like lemmings.

Ranger programs are often free, although in some units, or for some special programs, you may have to pay a few dollars per person.

Marsh-Billings-Rockefeller National Historical Park, for instance, Vermont's only NPS unit (apart from a section of the Appalachian National Trail), offers free admission to its 555 acres of re-planted and naturally regenerated woodlands in Woodstock, Vermont (not the location of the music festival! That's in New York State and is not an NPS unit). Marsh-Billings-Rockefeller does, however, make a small charge for some programs that take you into the park's mansion and focus on the contribution made to environmental conservation by the three families who lived on the estate over the past 200 years. The mansion also contains a rare collection of 19th century American landscape art from the Hudson River and Barbizon schools.

Ranger programs vary in capacity as well as content. Many can accommodate any number of people, and some only limited numbers, perhaps because the indoor spaces to be visited are small, because a vehicle can seat only a certain number of people, or because of impact on a natural area. Check ahead so you're not disappointed, or be prepared to be flexible!

For child-specific ranger program ideas, see Chapter 5: "Things To Do with Children and Grandchildren."

Visitor Centers

The Visitor Center (VC) is a mine of information. It's the place for finding out what's going on in the unit, whether it's a night sky expedition, a slideshow in the amphitheater, a chance to meet live birds of prey, or to watch a cow being milked by a costumed ranger.

Like spiders in the center of a web, the VC staff members sit at the nerve center of the visitor experience with restrooms, information, advice, exhibits, movies, and books for sale readily available. What more could you ask?

Not all VCs have everything of course, but in the bigger parks it can be hard to get out of them. Byrd Visitor Center at Big Meadows in Shenandoah National Park has all of the above, plus a large windowed area for viewing the Big Meadow itself, with its changing colors of vegetation, swooping barn swallows and bluebirds and hordes of white-tailed deer. It may sometimes take an effort of will to move beyond the VC!

Nor are all Visitor Centers the same. Private donations can lead to some interesting developments: The Laurance S. Rockefeller Preserve Center in Grand Tetons National Park, Wyoming, for instance, is a haven of quiet, peacefulness and gentle sensory experiences, reflecting the tastes of its donor, a person who was deeply committed to the philosophical and spiritual aspects of environmental conservation.

The Visitor Center is a good place to start your explorations.

CHAPTER 4: The Best Bargains

Fewer than one third of the 400-plus NPS units charge admission fees. Those that do, are not expensive. Some of the larger parks, for example, charge $30 for a carload of people – and the ticket usually lasts several days. Many ranger programs are free, although some units charge for specific programs, even if there's no entrance fee. Campgrounds usually charge modest per-night fees.

One of the reasons National Park units charge such low fees is that US citizens are already contributing to their budgets through their taxes. So that's another great reason to visit these places, and to make use of them – you're already paying for them!

At many of the smaller units – the ones that we're mostly talking about in this book – there is no entrance fee. But if you do go to the ones that charge admission, you'll want to know about the passes.

Discount Admission: Passes

The way to pay even less – to get the best bargains - is to obtain an "America the Beautiful" pass. There are a number of different ones for different groups of people: ordinary folks; 4th graders; seniors; people with disabilities; active military and their families and NPS volunteers with 250 service hours.

All passes in the "America the Beautiful" series offer a way to reduce the cost of visiting National Park units. The passes are terrific bargains if you're visiting several units that charge entrance fees, or if you're visiting the same fee-charging unit several times. Passes may be purchased in person at most federal recreation sites, by telephone at 1-888-275-8747, or online at *nps.gov. Details may change from time to time*

These passes aren't just for National Parks. Your pass admits you, and all passengers traveling in a private vehicle with you into a total of more than 2,000 federal fee-charging areas run by:

- National Park Service;
- National Forest Service;

- Fish and Wildlife Service;
- Bureau of Land Management;
- Bureau of Reclamation.

You need to know that:

When you use a pass for admission to an NPS unit, you must have the signed pass and your ID with you. There's no computer record, no way to look up the details at the Visitor Center or entrance station; so if you leave your pass at home, you have to pay admission, or buy a new one.

> Some units charge per person rather than per vehicle. In these the pass gives free admission for the pass holder and up to three other adults. Admission for kids 15 and under is free. ✑

In some places, like the White Mountain National Forest (part of the US Forest Service) in New Hampshire, you'll need a special hanger to display your pass in your parked vehicle while you go off hiking, photographing, bird watching, picnicking, or snoozing in the sunshine. Pick up the free hanger when you buy your pass.

Here are some details of the different passes:

Regular Annual Nationwide Family Vehicle Pass: $80

This is for regular folks, not yet 62, not in the 4th grade; not with a disability and not active military! It currently (2015) costs $80 and it's available to *anyone*, US citizen or not. And you can use it if you're on foot, horseback or bicycle too!

If you're going to several parks, especially big ones, you recoup the $80 cost of this pass pretty quickly, and after that it's all jam. If you're touring Arizona and Utah for instance:

- Petrified Forest $20;
- Grand Canyon $30;
- Bryce Canyon $30.

Total so far: $80. So any other fee-charging units you visit for *the rest of the year* can be considered free!

4th Grade Pass: Free

This pass gives 4th graders a chance to treat their families and friends to visits to National Park units. This pass lasts for the duration of your 4th grade school year and the following summer (September – August).

Tips

The annual America the Beautiful Pass is valid for one year from the month of issue. If you buy early in the month you get a little extra time: a pass bought on July 1, 2016 runs through July 31, 2017 – that's 13 months instead of 12!

These passes have space on the back for two signatures. The two people signing do not have to be related, so you can get extra value from this pass by having two families share it. You can buy a pass, sign just one of the spaces, and use the pass for your National Park trip, then share it with someone else who can sign the other space and use it for a separate trip.

You have to download a coupon from the "Every Kid in a Park" website, and take it to an NPS unit or other federal recreation site, where they'll exchange your coupon for a free pass. It qualifies for the same benefits as the regular pass.

Senior Pass

I've seen the visitors who arrive at an NPS unit on the morning of their 62nd birthday, waving a $10 bill and an ID in order to purchase the bargain of a lifetime: an America the Beautiful Senior Pass. The rangers may even sing "Happy Birthday". I've seen seniors' faces light up when they discover that for a mere $10 outlay they can

> **Why fourth-graders?**
>
> This pass is part of the White House "Every Kid in a Park" initiative. They reckon that 4th grade is a perfect moment to connect kids with nature; that many schools study state history in 4th grade and that it's logistically a good time to coordinate school field trips. ✎

get free admission to every NPS unit and lots of other federal lands for the *rest of their lives*. This is not an annual pass. As Ranger Kathleen tells people: "It expires when you do".

So here's the lowdown for the Senior Pass, bearing in mind that some details may change with time:

> *"It's very comforting to have the pass – anywhere I go I can just get in – it also feels as if I'm part of a community."*
>
> Senior Pass holder Evi, Washington D.C. ✎

- You have to be 62 or older;
- You have to be a US citizen or legal permanent resident;
- The pass may be purchased in person at an NPS unit, or purchased through the mail;
- It offers half price on federal camping fees;
- It costs $10 if you buy it in person, $20 if you buy it through the mail (2016 prices);

So what does this mean to you?

Say you and your friends, four adults altogether, decide to go to "red rock country" for a weekend and camp at Colorado National Monument in western Colorado in your RV or in tents. If one of you has the $10 Senior Pass, then, whatever the ages of the others, instead of paying the Monument's standard admission fee of $10 per vehicle you're in for free and ahead of the game already.

Sheep and Eagles

Colorado National Monument preserves 32 square miles of canyons and mesas in Colorado's Grand Valley, inhabited by desert bighorn and golden eagles. You can reach it from Interstate 70 via the towns of Fruita or Grand Junction. ⌒

Your pass then gives you half price on the campsite you secure for two nights: you pay $20 instead of $40. That's a total of $20 you've paid for admission and two nights camping that would have cost you $50 without the card. Even if you don't already have a pass but you buy it there and then, and count the full $10 cost of it, you're still saving $20 on your weekend.

At Joshua Tree National Park in southern California the same group would save paying the park's standard entrance fee of $20 per vehicle and then camp for $10 a night instead of $20. Sounds like cheap camping? Well, bear in mind that most National Park campgrounds are not fancy – they have only basic facilities.

Makes you want to get on the road, doesn't it? All you have to do is get there of course. If you live in the LA area, it's easy enough to get to Joshua Tree National Park – less than three hours east. From almost anywhere else it's a long haul, but well worth it for the rock climbing, spring wild flowers, and the tour of Keys Ranch (small fee charged), not to mention the Joshua Trees.

Joshua Trees

I thought I said not to mention them. Well, if we have to – they are fabulous! Someone thought they looked like the Old Testament character Joshua praying to God. All I can say is I'm sorry for any man that looks like that tree. They have bottle brush branches, grow to about 20 feet high and bear huge clusters of milky white flowers in March. To see a Joshua Tree inspires wonder at the fertile imagination of creation. Oh, and the flowers are fertilized by a specific type of moth that has co-evolved with the plant. ✎

Pass for People with Disabilities

If you have a permanent disability, your America the Beautiful pass is even cheaper; in fact, it's free. It's called an Access Pass. Once again you have to be a US citizen or legal permanent resident. You can buy the pass in person, or through the mail ($10 fee for this), if you provide proof of disability from your doctor, the VA, or a State agency. At some sites you may simply be asked to sign an affidavit that you have a qualifying disability.

Disability license plates or parking permits are not usually sufficient to qualify for this pass, because these are sometimes issued for temporary disabilities.

The Access Pass entitles you to all the same discounts as the Senior Pass, is good at all the same places, and also lasts for the rest of your life.

Pass for active duty US military and their dependents

This is an annual pass issued free to active duty US military personnel and their dependents. It gives free admission for the pass holder and passengers in a private non-commercial vehicle, or, in units that charge per person, free admission for the pass holder and up to three other adults.

You can pick one up in person at an NPS unit or other federal recreation area on production of military identification in the form of a CAC Card or DD Form 1173. (I expect you'll know what that is if you have one!)

Volunteer Pass

This free pass is issued as a thank you to volunteers who have donated a total of 250 volunteer hours to one of the participating federal agencies.

Site-Specific Annual Passes

Some NPS units or groups of units offer their own annual passes which give you unlimited entry for one year. This is great if you have a nearby unit you like to visit often, or a special unit you make several trips to every year. Muir Woods National Monument, in Mill Valley, near San Francisco, for instance, charges $20.00 for an annual pass. This admits the pass holder and up to three other adults. Since the normal daily fee for adult admission is $10 per person, this represents quite a saving.

Questions?

If you have questions about these passes, consult the trusty *nps.gov* website for full and current details.

Regular Entry Fees

If you don't use a pass and just pay a fee at the gate you'll find that most regular NPS unit vehicle-entry tickets are good for seven days, so if you're not over 62 and not visiting often, just staying near a single unit that you expect to visit several times during one week, buying the regular ticket may be the cheaper option.

You may find it encouraging to know that a large proportion of the entrance fee money collected at any one unit *stays at that unit* to fund projects and equipment. Some of the remainder of the fee money is shared with units that don't charge fees.

Children

The National Park Service wants as many youngsters as possible to visit and learn about these wonderful places, so 15-and-unders usually enjoy free admission to National Park units, although there may sometimes be a charge for children for specific programs at certain units. And don't forget the free 4th grade pass, which gets 4th-graders' families in free, too!!

How much more encouragement do you need to take the children or grandchildren? If you still need more, see Chapter 5.

Point Loma Lighthouse, Cabrillo National Monument,
San Diego, California

Discounts on Stuff!

At the Visitor Center bookstore in many NPS units, you can buy books, DVDs, posters, postcards, patches, and other useful and exciting items. These stores are usually run by a National Park Association, a non-profit "cooperating" organization that supports one or more National Park units in many wonderful ways. Just spending your money in these stores helps NPS units, and becoming an Association member helps even more!

Individual membership is usually about $30 a year. It entitles the member to a discount on goods in that Association's stores, and sometimes to discounts at commercially-run concerns within the unit.

Sometimes membership in one Association is honored by others, so you may be able to get discounts at other NPS units across the country. This varies, so you have to check it out depending on where you join and where you wish to shop.

As well as the non-profit Association stores, there may be gift stores, restaurants and lodgings within NPS units that are run by commercial concession holders. They, too, sometimes offer some discounts to Association members, so remember to ask!

And, don't forget, your Association membership and purchases support the NPS!

Free Admission on Special Days!

The National Park Service offers free admission to all units nationwide on several special days and weekends every year, and even on five consecutive days in April during "National Parks Week". Exact dates vary from year to year, so check these on *nps.gov* by querying "fee free days". ✑

CHAPTER 5: Things to Do with Children and Grandchildren

What a fantastic time you can have in NPS units with children, seeing history come to life, exploring specific aspects of life in the USA, spotting birds and flowers, walking in the rain, or learning how to cope with camping!

How special it is for children – maybe one at a time - to have an adventure with parents or grandparents in an NPS unit! Bear in mind that an adventure for a small child can be as simple as watching busy ants on an ant hill, seeing dinosaur fossils, or finding out that people used to live in cliff dwellings.

So, find the one or two nearest NPS units to your home or wherever you go on vacation with your family, and check out the action. Just being in these places, hanging out and exploring, can be neat. There's a lot to learn too, and a lot of special fun to be had.

Junior Rangers

More than 300 NPS units offer self-directed Junior Ranger program booklets, free or costing a few dollars, that contain a range of activities to be completed in order to qualify as a "Junior Ranger", a young steward of our heritage.

The booklets are suitable usually for children aged 5 to 14. When they complete the number of activities specified for their age and maybe attend a ranger program, each child receives a certificate and a badge or patch. Park staff will try to make the time to discuss with the child the work she or he has done in the Junior Ranger booklet, and to hold a little "investiture" ceremony before presenting the badge.

A few units have extended the age range of their Junior Ranger programs to include material suitable for younger children and for older teenagers. Some adults, too, find that doing the Junior Ranger booklet is a great way to get to know a unit.

The John Fitzgerald Kennedy National Historic Site, in Brookline, Massachusetts, for example, provides each aspiring Junior Ranger with a booklet, clipboard, and pencil. They have a yellow-star booklet for 5-to-8-year olds, and a red-star booklet for 9-to-12-year olds.

Bandelier National Monument in Los Alamos, New Mexico, offers three different Junior Ranger worksheets for pre-K through 6th grade, and a "Deputy Ranger" worksheet for 7th grade and up, including adults!

It doesn't end there, though. Junior Ranger booklets usually contain more challenges than necessary to get the badge, so children may have some pages still to finish – a good occupation for the journey home or a subsequent rainy day.

If you don't have time to finish the required number of Junior Ranger activities on one visit to the unit, that's a good reason for a second visit. If there isn't going to be a next time, then you may be able to work on the rest of the required pages at home and mail the booklet to the unit; if it's been adequately completed, they'll mail you the badge.

Girl Scout and Boy Scout Rangers can earn a handsome patch by participating for ten hours or more in an organized educational activity, or

Get ahead

Many units post their Junior Ranger booklets online so you can download one before you visit if you wish to get a head start. ✎

volunteering in a National Park unit. Plus, National Park units can be great places for individual Scouts and troops of Scouts to work on merit badges like Hiking, Cooking, Backpacking, Orienteering and Citizenship in the Community.

Web Rangers: the online version

Computer-savvy youngsters will enjoy the NPS WebRangers site. It's one of the very best on the Internet for interesting, interactive, educational activities. Find it at *http://www. webrangers.us* (don't just enter "WebRangers" in a search engine – you'll get the cartoon Power Rangers!) or go to *nps. gov* and search.

The site is super: it's fun, varied, stimulates thought, and there's no advertising. The summer my grandson Damon was ten, he worked his way through it on rainy days and evenings and completed all 47 (at that time) challenges. They range from code breaking to exploring tide pools, hunting for whale knowledge and following the adventures of westward-bound railroads. Challenges are rated easy, medium and difficult, and you earn a patch for your online camp blanket for each one you complete.

If your children log in to WebRangers, they'll have hours of self-directed, educational fun and come away with a sense of achievement. It says it's for "children of all ages". I'd say the operating level is around 4th to 6th grade. Younger children could do some with adult help, but, hey, I think it's much better to find age-appropriate activities so that the child can shine.

Virtual Junior Rangers

Some units also have their own virtual Junior Ranger program. These are different from the WebRangers – they're usually downloadable quiz sheets that can be mailed in to obtain a badge and certificate.

Among those offering such a program is Eisenhower National Historic Site in Gettysburg, Pennsylvania, which has a print-out Junior Secret Service Manual on its web page for kids to work through and mail in for their badge and certificate. Other Units with online Junior Ranger activities include Tonto National Monument in Arizona; Point Reyes National Seashore in California; Denali National Park and Preserve in Alaska; and the Lewis and Clark National Historic Trail which winds its way across 11 states from Indiana to Washington.

The NPS home page at *nps.gov* also offers interactive activities for all ages, such as an e-hike in Sequoia National Park or webcams at Rocky Mountain National Park.

Junior Ranger Programs offered in the Units

Back on the ground at the unit, there may be ranger-led Junior Ranger programs for children accompanied by an adult. These typically last one-and-a-half to two hours. They may offer completely different activities from the self-directed booklet, or they might work through the booklet, or focus on one activity in it. To find times of Junior Ranger and all other ranger programs, check online, look in the unit's newspaper or other publication, check out the notice boards, or ask at the Visitor Center.

If you're checking online it's especially important to be sure you're on the official NPS web site at *nps.gov*. As I mentioned in Chapter I, there are copycat sites and they can give incorrect information.

Junior Ranger programs are usually not drop-off programs: they may require an adult to stay with the children so that they can work together. If the program says it's for 7-to-12-year-olds, don't expect that your 5-year-old is going to be able to fully participate. Rangers are infinitely patient and usually don't mind young children being brought along with an older sibling, but the ranger's job is to run a program appropriate for the advertised age group, so she usually can't adapt it fully to someone outside the age range. Younger children get their chance too, at some units, with shorter "Kiddies Corner" programs or similar offerings. There may also be self-guided children's activities available in the Visitor Center. Take a good look round!

Annually, during National Park Week, which is held in April, there's a Junior Ranger Day when many units make a special effort to come up with something new and creative and to draw in youngsters and their families. Look out for this! Check it out online or at your local unit! Bear in mind that some northern parks don't start their ranger program season until later in the year.

*Sand sledding in June at White Sands National Monument,
New Mexico*

Ranger Programs in general – is there a place for children?

Ranger-led programs are an important and traditional part of the National Park experience. Take your children to ranger programs and they'll learn social skills like paying attention and asking relevant questions, as well as discovering amazing facts about bears, eagles, flintlock pistols, Native American homes, Lincoln's death mask, monarch butterflies, and the Battle of Gettysburg. The aim of the programs is, however, not to fill heads with facts – it's to open people's eyes and help them to think about, feel, and connect with the meanings of these places and the natural and cultural history they protect – isn't that a wonderful gift to give your children?

The visitor group will normally be very mixed and the rangers are skilled in the art of providing something for everyone, so the ranger programs are often great for young children, parents, and everyone in between. They are, however, hugely varied in content, duration and degree of activity required; many are suitable for all ages, but do make sure you know what's on the agenda before you turn up with young children!

The programs are designed to help people connect with all aspects of the units, so some involve difficult hiking terrain, squeezing through narrow openings in caves, scrambling over rocks, keeping quiet and sitting still to watch wildlife, taking turns, listening, holding back questions until an appropriate moment, and, heaven help us, even thinking!

The Grandparent Connection

A large proportion of NPS visitors every year are from the "Baby Boom" generation. That, according to the US Census Bureau, includes anyone born between 1946 and 1965 – quite a wide range.

Judging by the statistics, Baby Boomers appreciate NPS units. They are also the current "grandparent" generation, so there's an equation to be made here, I think!

Grandparents are in a wonderful position to use their love for and knowledge of National Park units to benefit future generations rather than "just" enhancing their own lives. These places are tailor-made for grandparents and children to enjoy together.

How great it is to give parents a break – taking one, two, three, however many you wish, of the children off their hands. It's a win-win-win-win-win situation:

- grandparents enjoy time with their grandchildren;
- children have a memorable experience;
- parents get time to paint the living room;
- the NPS chalks up more visitors;
- the younger generation begins to care about and care for these wonderful places.

Yay!!

Schools Programs

Teachers, school superintendents, PTA members: if your school isn't already working with your nearest National Park property, call them and find out what's available. NPS units all over the country offer curriculum-based programs, classroom visits, opportunities to participate in ongoing projects and professional development for teachers. Their resources can be alternative indoor and outdoor classrooms for teachers to use creatively.

And the resources provided by National Park units can be goldmines for homeschooling families, too.

ॐ

CHAPTER 6: The Reassurance Chapter

A visit to a presidential library, an historic house, a 19th century ironworks, or a well-signposted Civil War battlefield may not offer any unusual physical challenges. There are, however, some important things to remember during exploration of these special places.

National Park units are there to stimulate and provoke as well as to entertain and inspire. They help us think about nature, history, culture and the environment; they prompt us to learn, to remember, to enjoy, to connect and to pass on our enthusiasms, ideas and knowledge. Spending time visiting these places feeds the intellect, the imagination, and the human spirit. That means that to get the best out of them we have to engage – to open our minds, to think.

Does that sound scary? Or difficult? Or exciting? I hope so! This chapter includes some things to consider when engaging!

Historic buildings in National Park Service units often house collections of exquisite porcelain, paintings, furniture and other artifacts.

Physical Well Being

Many of the National Park properties, the "Treasures On Your Doorstep", that I'm talking about in this book, are urban. The hazards they present are those negotiated daily by urban dwellers, who do, after all, make up the majority of our population. There's not much in the way of hazards at, for instance, a place like the Herbert Hoover National Historic Site in West Branch, Iowa, where visitors can see the birthplace of the 31st President and visit his presidential library. Other units, however, are wild and wonderful, perhaps more in line with the classic concept of "a national park". So let's take a few minutes to consider safety in natural areas like Bighorn Canyon National Recreation Area in the northern Rockies or a National Seashore like Cape Cod.

Life is for living: there are, of course, hazards associated with everything we do, and it's up to us to understand them. Most accidents happen in our own homes – well, after all, we spend a lot of time there! And driving or traveling in an automobile is a very risky thing to do; you'd be unusual if you don't personally know someone – a friend or relative – who's been injured in a car crash, yet most of us continue to travel in cars, often very fast.

This illustrates the concept of "acceptable level of risk". We each have a different degree of risk we're prepared to accept in our lives, depending on the perceived advantage. Thus, we might normally cross a busy road only on a crosswalk, but fear of being late for an important appointment might lead us to take our lives in our hands and cross in the midst of heavy traffic.

Similarly, many aspects of National Park units are very safe, and some are some exciting, even scary. The Angels Landing hike in Zion National Park, Utah, for example, with its stomach-churning sheer drops on either side is not for everyone, although thousands of people successfully and happily – well, some of them happily (not me!) - negotiate it every year.

Taking care

Historic houses, farms, settlements, and urban trails are pretty safe for most people, but if you look at the other side of the coin, we, the people, can present hazards for historic structures and artifacts;

The key to safety and to treating historic sites with respect is personal awareness. In this as in all things, taking responsibility for ourselves and being conscious of our effect on our surroundings is absolutely the key to success.

Respect for Artifacts

When I say that we can present hazards to cultural and historical treasures, this is what I mean:

- Everything that is part of the National Park units belongs to the people of the United States;
- We may wish to see all these wonderful pieces of history preserved for our grandchildren and great grandchildren to see, learn about, and wonder at;
- Paintings, adobe walls, ceramics, carpets and books can all be damaged by touching because our hands, however clean, have natural oils and bacteria on them which break down the microscopic structure of items we touch;
- Museum staff avoid touching artifacts unnecessarily, and when they do have to handle items they wear clean white gloves;
- We can cause mechanical damage as well as chemical, because the friction of touching abrades surfaces;
- Thousands of small touches over many years add up to erosion and degradation;
- Yes, fungal spores and bacteria in the air, mice and insects on the ground, and acid rain also cause deterioration to structures and objects – but why add to it? Why not do what we can to preserve these objects?
- So, if you want to preserve our historic legacy for the future, if you're asked not to touch - don't touch!
- Everything in the park stays in the park! This includes walking sticks, pretty rocks, Indian artifacts, flowers and earthworms!

In the built as well as in the natural environment, awareness is the name of the game. You may feel a natural urge to run your hand over a beautiful old chair, but it's an urge to be resisted. The alternative is for all these things to be put behind glass.

If you spot an artifact from historic or prehistoric times when you're out hiking, please just leave it where it is. Take all the photos you wish – but don't even touch it! Touching or moving artifacts puts them out of context and makes it much harder for archeologists to gather information.

Park staff members try to keep the built and the natural environments and everything in them in good condition, as far as budgets allow, to be handed on to generations to come. We visitors can help with this work by following rules and recommendations, even checking them out before we visit.

Balance and care is the Park Service's job; awareness and care is ours.

Dangerous Terrain?

Many National Monuments, Recreation Areas and other units offer hiking trails, and they'll usually rate them roughly according to difficulty. If in doubt about the suitability of a hike, ask the staff – they're there to help you, and they often have personal experience of the trails.

You can check the unit's webpage ahead of time for a suitable hike, and even download maps or route guides.

You know that you'd be foolish to attempt anything more than a very short, level walk wearing flip-flops and not carrying water, don't you? Remember that if it's downhill on the way out, it's going to be uphill on the way back, so you need to conserve some energy for your return.

If you climb on boulders or rock faces, you can slip and fall off. Stay within the range of your own ability and always remember that whatever you do, wherever you go, you want to be able to get back under your own steam, without calling out search parties and helicopters. Look ahead, and if you're getting on in life, remember, we're not as young as we once were. With increasing age, however, comes increasing wisdom – that's why most of the people rescue parties have to go out after are youngsters!

Sturdy shoes or hiking boots, particularly those that snuggle cozily around your ankles, giving support to that delicate mechanism, are desirable for long walks, and any walks on uneven and rocky terrain. Hiking poles are a wonderful invention that can be used to relieve weight on knees when going downhill. Don't eschew poles as a sign of age or incapacity; many of the very fit people who through-hike the 2,000-mile Appalachian National Scenic Trail swing along using two hiking poles! The AT, by the way, is a National Park unit. It spans 14 states from Georgia to Maine - or the other way round, if you prefer!

You may very well find yourself alone on a trail: most people don't venture far away from parking areas and Visitor Centers, and National Park units can be in remote or mountainous places where cell phone reception is patchy. Cell phones, incidentally, are said to have changed people's behavior when lost. In the past, the advice was always to head downhill, find a stream or gully and follow it to civilization. Nowadays, because cell phone reception can be poor if it's blocked by mountains, lost people head for the highest point they can find, in order to get cell reception and call for help.

What to take

My carry list for a day hike or a long walk depends on where I am, and the time of year. Here's a rough guide:

- Water: never stray far without this, and remember that drinking from wild streams or ponds is a no-no, because of the animal life in them, microscopic and otherwise. If you're out for a long time and need to use wild water, carry a filter or purifying tablets, or both. However, desert parks may ask you not to drink any wild water, but rather to leave it for the animals;
- Food: even if you're not planning on picnicking during your hike, have something stashed away for emergencies – maybe a couple of energy bars in case you flag on the way back, or meet a starving stranger;
- Sunblock: protect your skin year-round; it has to last a lifetime – skin cancer is on the increase, especially among young people. It's a good idea to make a habit of using

sunblock as moisturizer before venturing out on sunny days. Remember that the reflective effects of water and snow intensify the potency of the sun's rays;

- Map: take one of your specific trail as well as the unit and the area in general;

- Hand-held GPS unit if you have one – and know how to use it! Same goes for compass and map – make sure you know how to use them!

- First-aid kit: never go anywhere without Band-Aids! Antiseptic wipes and something soothing for plant stings and insect bites can be useful unless you're good at the wild lore of plant remedies;

- Extra clothing: take another layer in case it gets cooler. The clothing makes useful padding in your day pack, anyway;

- Weather gear: as appropriate: a sun hat in the south; a light raincoat in temperate zones; woolly hat and gloves if it's a beautiful October day and you're going to be gaining elevation;

- Plastic shopping bags: for picking up odd bits of litter – thank you! Ranger John calls plastic shopping bags "portable lawn chairs" because they're useful for sitting on in damp places!

- Eyeglasses, if you wear them: a pair and a spare - you want to be able to read the map, and look closely at flowers, rocks and lichen;

- Whistle: get one, stick it in the backpack and forget it. If you ever do get lost, it could save your bacon;

- Optional: camera and spare batteries; binoculars; field guides – cell phone e-field guide apps are great, if you're in cellphone range!

Weather

Weather can be changeable. Check it out online before you leave home. Check it on the car radio as you travel. Check it at the entrance station or Visitor Center when you arrive.

Remember that weather changes with elevation. Driving up into the mountains may mean driving up into a cloud, and is usually going to mean driving up to a lower temperature. Setting out on a warm October day to hike uphill, you may be hiking into winter.

Proper Preparation

- Research your route and its terrain;
- Plan carefully to allow enough time;
- Tell someone where you're going;
- Leave a nice flask of hot tea or coffee, or some cold drinks, in the car for when you return;
- Keep Epsom salts at home for the reviving bath.

Water and Other Features – e.g. Geysers!

Water is the staff of life, and in quantity it can be the stuff of death. Sounds ominous? Well, adventurous or foolish people can get into trouble, especially with water sports. Water-related fatalities happen in NPS units every year. And the super-heated waters of the Yellowstone geysers are lethal – stay a safe distance! That reminds me of a good idea – take note of warning signs: they're there for a reason!

Staying Un-Lost and Getting Found

There are two big issues here: how to not get lost in the first place, and how to find yourself, or be found, once you are lost.

Prevention being better than cure, we'll think about not getting lost in the first place.

Plan Ahead

- Tell someone who cares where you're going and what time you expect to return;
- Craft your itinerary to fit your abilities and those of your companions;
- Get a map ahead of time, study it, take it with you, and use it;
- Even before that, learn to read a map and use a compass or a GPS unit – these can be great activities for cold, snowy, and rainy days. They can also be fun things to do with children or grandchildren. Map, compass, and GPS use has to be learned – we're not born with instinctive knowledge of how to do these things.

If You Do Get Lost

Everyone gets lost sometimes; it's part of life. Getting lost can happen at all sorts of levels: being confronted with a family situation in which you don't know how to feel; tackling a work problem where you can't see the route to the solution, and, what we're talking about here, being physically lost in the landscape.

The Hitchhikers' Guide to the Galaxy (*created by Douglas Adams*) is a fictional book with a very useful motto printed across its cover in large letters: ***"DON'T PANIC"***. Does that help?

Maybe, because after all, a calm appraisal of the situation is called for when you realize you're lost. Whoa – let's step back a bit. The first thing is to admit that you are lost. This can be hard: some of us find it harder than others!

- Pause; take a deep breath and a drink of water because you know that preventing dehydration is better than remedying it!
- If separated from the rest of your party, yell, whistle, then stop and listen;
- Check your surroundings, pick something nearby that you can recognize at a distance, like a tall dead tree so that you will be able to return to the last known point;
- Explore carefully for a way out;
- Check your own pulse to make sure you're not being hasty. Be ready to wait out the night if you have no light. Even with a light, travel at night can be risky;
- Should you have to find or make a shelter, or gather firewood, do it before dark or before the storm arrives.

If You Can't Find Your Own Way Out

- Stay near an open area, for visibility;
- Make a signal: a brightly-colored pack, artificial patterns such as tracks in the snow, a signal mirror (this is a special type of

mirror, not just any one, although any one might work in a fix), a flashlight, aerial flare, fire at night or smoke by day.

If a Member of Your Party Is Missing

- Search for them, but preserve tracks and any articles like clothing or other belongings that carry their scent. Note witnesses, point-last-seen, locations of camps and cars;
- Send for help, with a clear, complete, accurate report, including all relevant information.

Wildlife Hazards
Noxious Plants

Some of the more common irritant plants you might encounter while hiking, especially if you go off trail, are poison ivy, wood nettles and European stinging nettles, poison oak, poison sumac, and wild parsnip.

You can do a great deal to keep yourself safe from the skin irritations caused by these plants.

- Make sure before you set out that you know what you might encounter, and that you know how to identify possible irritants;
- Stay on trails - such plants will generally have been cleared away from trails regularly used by people;
- Protect your skin with long sleeves and, especially, long pants or gaiters;

- Don't touch suspect or unidentified plants;
- Carry an antidote or soothing lotion in your pack. Fels Naptha soap is the best remedy I know for poison ivy – wash the affected area and clothing to remove the noxious oil. Many supermarkets stock Fels Naptha in the detergent aisle;
- Ask. The park staff will know if there's a hazard on a particular trail or at a particular time of year.

Venomous Snakes

With snakes, it's once again a question of acceptable level of risk and personal responsibility. People will scoff at your fears of being bitten by a venomous snake and tell you: "You have a much greater chance of being hit by a car in your own neighborhood than of being bitten by a venomous snake," or "Very few people die of snake bites in the USA!" True: however, situations alter statistics, and one of the few places you are more likely to be bitten by a venomous snake than be hit by a car is on a steep rocky hiking trail in the Mojave Desert, far from any road. Even so, it's very unlikely to happen. Most of the people who get bitten do so because they try to pick up or otherwise antagonize the snake.

Snakes play a very important role in the environment. They're a vital part of the food chain, eating countless small rodents and in turn, being eaten by larger animals, even humans. A snake is one long sinuous muscle and that means meat!

Snakes are beautiful. Next time you have a chance to see one close up – in the zoo or science center perhaps – look long and hard at the exquisite shading and coloration of the scales, the way they overlap one another, the supple movements. If you can see the underside of the snake you'll marvel at the difference of the scales there – in cross section a snake is not round but flat-bottomed, like a loaf of bread.

Looking at the scales on the lower part of the underside of the tail is a good way to tell venomous and non-venomous snakes apart. The venomous ones have a single row of scales here and the others have a double row – or perhaps it's the other way round – who the heck is ever going to look?

Seriously, though, the best way to avoid venomous snakes is to avoid any snake. There seem always to be exceptions to rules about identifying them. So, for instance, non-venomous snakes have round pupils to their eyes, while venomous ones have slit-shaped pupils. Except, that is, for the ones that don't, like the venomous although reclusive coral snake, which has round pupils.

Many venomous snakes have triangular heads, large enough to accommodate venom pouches, but several species of non-venomous snake can mimic this head shape, changing even as you watch them. Some harmless snakes mimic rattlesnakes by vibrating their tails among dead leaves to cause a rattling sound. While harmless snakes imitating venomous ones are not going to hurt you, their behavior illustrates that in the wild, things are not always what they seem to be, so stay clear and stay safe!

Venomous vs. Poisonous

Let's be precise in our use of language: snakes are venomous, deadly nightshade is poisonous.

The difference is that venom is injected – from a snake's fangs, and poison is ingested – taken in through the mouth (or ear in the case of Hamlet's father). ◈

So you're not going to be handling a live snake in the wild at all, because they all can bite, and any bites can carry germs! Don't pick up a "dead" snake either! Post mortem muscular contractions could bring you into contact with a fang, or the creature may not really be dead at all: snakes are cold-blooded and become torpid or immobile in cold temperatures.

But this isn't a natural history book: the question is how to avoid snake encounters. The answer is awareness, being in the present. Ranger Ken says: "Watch where you put your hands, your feet, and your seat!" Never, never, never, when scrambling up rocks or pulling weeds, put your hands or any other part of your body down unless you can see that the place is clear.

Sticking to trails helps, because then you can see where you're putting your feet. Bushwhacking is more dangerous.

If you're privileged to see one of these fascinating creatures, stop and enjoy the sight from a safe distance. Snakes have featured in our stories from the earliest times, and not always in a negative way: look at Kaa in Rudyard Kipling's "Jungle Book", which, incidentally, I recommend reading. Ignore the movie, that's a parody.

Young black bear in the Blue Ridge Mountains of Virginia

Charismatic Megafauna

NPS units where there is a chance of encountering large and impressive animals – sometimes referred to as "charismatic megafauna" - will usually provide lots of advice and warnings.

Forget about Yogi Bear and feeding the animals – it's not only unwise and illegal, it's unfair to the animals themselves. Deer and bears that come to rely on or expect human food become habituated to humans and cars, and run the risk of injury because they don't get out of the way quickly enough.

They can also become a nuisance and a danger to people. If you feed a deer some potato chips, what happens when you come to the end of the bag? The deer doesn't know why the food has stopped and it's going to want more. It may start pushing at you. Deer can pack a hefty and damaging kick if they feel threatened or upset. They can kill dogs!

Habituated "nuisance" animals, those who've become used to begging for human food, eventually have to be trapped and relocated, or even euthanized.

And you can expose yourself to suspicion by feeding wild animals, because that's what poachers do, enabling them to kill a habituated deer as it comes up alongside the truck looking for food.

If you're heading into an area where you might encounter large animals, check in with the Visitor Center about ways to stay safe and not frighten the animals or impinge on their habitat.

Solo Visiting

Do you find it hard to go to a new place alone? Perhaps you don't even think of visiting historic sites unless you have someone to accompany you. Quite honestly, I've sometimes found that if I wait until I find someone to do something with me, I may never get to do it; so I just pick up and do it alone. I learn a lot more that way because I can focus on nature and the history of the site without the diversion of interacting with other people. I've met some interesting people that way, too – some of them quoted in this book.

Take the bull by the horns and go alone – perhaps you're checking the place out to see if the grandchildren would enjoy it. This is your park and there's no rule that says you have to have someone with you to visit and enjoy. There are advantages to solo visiting, too.

Solo Hiking

Adults can make their own decisions about whether to hike alone. It's a question of acceptable levels of risk. Of course it's riskier than hiking with a companion, because if you get hurt there's no-one to send for help. On the other hand,

Stephen from Portland, Oregon, found that being alone paid off at Craters of the Moon National Monument and Preserve in Idaho: *"As often happens when you're by yourself, I had a special experience. I was hiking across a broken lava field when I saw a badger – I've never seen one before or since – what a surprise to come round a corner and see a large mammal like that scurrying away. It's the treat that you may find by being quiet and alone."*

if you prepare properly and stick to established trails you're as safe as walking a city street – maybe safer.

The huge advantage to hiking alone is the opportunity it gives you to move at your own pace, stop whenever you want to, stay silent among the natural wildness, think, meditate, empty your mind, drink in the glories of nature, get to know yourself, work out issues, rehearse speeches, and have imaginary conversations. I think you can tell that I'm a fan of solo hiking.

Firearms

The bottom line with personal firearms in NPS units since February 2010 is that people who can legally possess firearms under applicable federal, state, and local laws, can also legally possess firearms in NPS units, in compliance with those local laws. That means that, with one exception, there are usually no *special* laws governing firearm possession within NPS units – the laws are the same as in the surrounding state, county or municipality. *It's up to the user to check out and know those laws* – as anyone carrying a firearm always should, of course.

Where the NPS departs from local laws is that most of the buildings in NPS units are federally owned, and federal law prohibits possession of personal firearms in federal buildings. So you cannot legally take a personal firearm into the Visitor Center or, usually, into any other building in any NPS unit.

About 70 NPS units, ten of them in Alaska, allow hunting. They include the Mojave National Preserve in California, the Little River Canyon National Preserve in Alabama, and the Big Cypress National Preserve in Florida. Regulations vary: be sure you know them before setting out to hunt.

CHAPTER 7: Participation

*"T*hese parks are my parks; these parks are your parks" – with apologies to Woody Guthrie.

We can all visit and enjoy the park units, large and small, on our doorsteps or far away – and there are many ways of becoming a part of what author Wallace Stegner dubbed "the best idea we ever had".

Volunteering

Many of the people you'll encounter in NPS units are volunteers. If you look closely you may find the word "volunteer" written somewhere on their uniform, although not all of them are in uniform. The incognito ones are likely to be the valiant invasive plant pullers, the invaluable volunteer naturalists, the bird counters, the leaflet distributors, the photographers, the office volunteers and other behind-the-scenes workers helping with research, special projects or day-to-day chores.

The more visible volunteers will be those who interact with visitors: maybe campground hosts or Visitor Center volunteers.

John and Eileen explained their urge to volunteer as campground hosts like this:

"We love the national parks and think they are to be cherished by all. We volunteer because we can. It's a wonderful way to contribute to the parks and to be immersed for a few months in these exceptional sites."

Sometimes the volunteer opportunity picks the person:

"Two park rangers who noticed that I was doing a lot of hiking in the park suggested I put my knowledge to use to help visitors," explained Keith, who volunteers in an NPS unit in California.

He had more advice to offer: *"A good volunteer experience happens when you're doing something you like, so find the task that's right for you. If you're a people person, help out in the Visitor Center, roam the trails, or lead programs for groups. If you prefer behind-the-scenes work, help out in the office or museum.*

"Volunteering in a National Park unit is exciting, and you're guaranteed to see new things every time you go in, whether volunteering or hiking on your own. Don't let the rough days get you down.

"This next advice is from when I volunteered in a hospital years ago: keep on rockin', even when you don't feel appreciated. (Some of those doctors could be mean to volunteers) .... Good karma will roll back around to you... it may take a while, but it will happen."

Volunteering is a part of the American way of life, and the National Park Service doesn't recruit volunteers just to fill gaps in its staffing. It has a positive commitment to offering people opportunities for volunteering. It's a very positive partnership. More than 220,000 people volunteer in National Park units each year. Through 2008, a cumulative total of 2,482,104 people had volunteered in National Parks units (information from *http://www.nps.gov*). By comparison, the NPS employs about 20,000 staff members at any one time.

The NPS's central volunteer program is called VIP – Volunteers in Parks – and many units use this system. To find volunteer opportunities, call or email the park of your choice and ask to be put in touch with the volunteer coordinator. If you're interested in a number of different parks, or you need to have your appetite sharpened, you can browse opportunities at *http://www.nps.gov/getinvolved/volunteer.htm.*

Student Conservation Association

Volunteering can be a stepping stone to permanent employment in the NPS, and one very well-oiled route to this is through an internship with the Student Conservation Association – the SCA. No, you don't have to be a student, and you can be any age to become an intern, from teenager to senior. This amazing organization, headquartered in Arlington, VA, was the brainchild of Liz Putnam who, in 1955, wrote a thesis outlining a "Student Conservation Corps" modeled after the Civilian Conservation Corps which did so much sterling work in National Parks in the 1930s.

The SCA has grown to encompass many different programs. In 2014 it found opportunities for more than 7,500 volunteers and interns to serve in hundreds of natural and cultural sites, including many NPS units, in all 50 states. It provides members with hands-on conservation service opportunities in virtually every field imaginable, from tracking grizzlies through the Tetons to restoring desert ecosystems to teaching environmental education at Washington D.C.'s Urban Tree House.

SCA provides a great volunteer opportunity that is invaluable to the park units. What's more, an estimated 12 percent of National Park Service employees got their start with SCA, according to *nps.gov*. Find this organization at www.*thesca.org*.

Internships are sponsored by many other organizations and by individual parks, too. Here are a few:

- GeoCorps, a program of the Geological Society of America: *http://rock.geosociety.org*
- The National Parks Conservation Association in Washington DC recruits interns to work on community organizing and legislative lobbying: *www.npca.org*
- The National Park Foundation, the fund-raising non-profit partner of the NPS, offers internships in marketing, communications, and development in Washington DC: *www.nationalparks.org*
- The Golden Gate National Parks Conservancy is an example of a partnership organization serving one or several individual units. It offers internship opportunities at 29 national and state parks in the San Francisco area, including Alcatraz, Muir Woods National Monument, and Point Reyes National Seashore: *http://www. parksconservancy.org*

Some internship programs are very specific: Yosemite Leadership Program internships, for instance, are available only to University of California, Merced, undergraduates.

There's even a scuba-diving internship with the NPS underwater branch!

There could very well be a place for you or a member of your family on an internship program in a national park unit!

Employment

One of the biggest commitments you could make is actually to work for the National Park Service. An internship can help to open doors to employment, and there are other ways of getting a job, too. Applying is a good start. Where to apply? Take a look at the federal government's job page *usajobs.gov* Remember, as with *nps.gov*, the ".gov" is crucial because there are copy-cat sites.

Applying for government jobs, including NPS jobs, is a lengthy and complicated process, so be prepared to put some effort into it ("give it some welly," the Brits would say).

An entire book could be written on applying for NPS jobs – maybe I'll do that next. For now, I'll just say that you need to construct an extensive online resume, far longer and more detailed than any resume you would send to a private company, and you need to monitor new postings to the site weekly if not daily. You can sign up to have job vacancy lists emailed to you.

Federal jobs are sometimes advertised in local and professional media too. Wherever they're advertised and for whatever discipline, there's usually stiff competition and, as it's federal employment, military veterans are entitled to preferential consideration.

Cricket player at English Camp, San Juan Island National Historical Park, Washington

A park superintendent once told me that he thought working for the NPS is "honorable employment". I think he meant that the work contributes to the general good, so an employee can feel proud or at least content to be doing it. That's got to be worth something to an individual.

There are many, many different types of jobs within the NPS, including law enforcement rangers who are police officers; fee collectors; maintenance personnel; resource scientists, historians; administrators; attorneys; human relations and public relations staff; interpretive rangers; trail crews and managers.

One visitor found out about one sort of job available in the NPS when he visited John Day Fossil Beds National Monument in Oregon:

> "As I pulled into the parking lot a ranger car drew up. I wasn't quite sure what was going on: had I done something wrong? But I talked to the ranger and it turned out that she was an entomologist come to survey butterflies. I asked if I could tag along.

> "Once you become aware and start to track butterflies there are so many more than you expect. Having a conversation with someone who's endeavoring to track the condition of the environment by surveying for butterflies was a real eye-opener. Here

*was someone you never hear about, never expect to
meet."*

Rangers' jobs are indeed varied, as John, a schoolteacher
from Rutland, Vermont, found out:

> *"It was amazing: here was this ranger who looked as
> if she was going to take us on a hike – when we walked
> into the mansion she started talking about Art!"*

In addition to permanent jobs, there are many seasonal
opportunities where people are employed for a few months
at a time. Park units have busy seasons and need to staff up
for the summer or winter rush like any other tourism enter-
prise, so many of the rangers you meet are temporary workers.
It's a bit like being an office temp with the most glorious or
fascinating office in the world!

Finding a Treasure and a Job

Iraq veteran Jason was retiring after 28 years in the US
Army when he discovered the treasure on *his* doorstep.

> *"The closest National Park unit was three miles
> from home and I didn't know it was there – it was
> a kind of secret,"* he said. *"I was born in the area
> and my parents lived there, but we didn't know it
> was there."*

The treasure Jason found was Prince William Forest Park, originally established in 1936 as the Chopawamsic National Recreational Demonstration Area. It's in Virginia, just 35 miles from the nation's capital and it was set up during the Great Depression to provide a breath of fresh area for the people of that fair city.

A chance visit to Prince William changed Jason's life: *"In the Visitor Center I picked up a kid's book called "Would you like to be a Park Ranger" and every page I looked at I thought: "I'd like to do that!" The ranger behind the desk encouraged me – I didn't think it was possible to be a park ranger because I didn't have the background."*

It turned out to be very possible. Starting out as a volunteer – a job that included collecting scat for a carnivore study – Jason was soon taken on as a seasonal park ranger. For two summer seasons he prepared and presented interpretive programs as well as carrying on with the duties he'd had as a volunteer: yes, more scat-collecting!

Moving to the Mid-West, he found a new seasonal position at a National Monument. He'd always enjoyed visiting the parks, and now he's part of the scenery: *"I loved it right from the beginning,"* he said. *"I took to it like a duck to water."*

Commercial Concessions

Within many parks are concessions, including hotels, restaurants, lodges and trail-riding stables, run by commercial companies large and small, and employment with these, mostly seasonal, is another good way to spend time inside a park. Some people return year after year to a favorite park this way.

Other involvement: Donating

Financial help is always useful.

We US taxpayers all support the NPS through our tax dollars, and as visitors we chip in with the fees we pay to enter the park units, use their campgrounds and sometimes pay for programs. Preserving and conserving the nation's natural and cultural treasures is a huge job, however, and there's never enough money for all the wonderful projects that could be done. So straightforward donations are a great way to add to your support for this work – remember, you can make donations during your lifetime or posthumously in your will!

Many units have donation boxes in the Visitor Center, and the entire contents of the donation box usually stay in that unit – the wider organization doesn't get its hands on it! Staff members don't accept tips, so if you've loved the ranger program, or someone's been helpful with advice and directions, and want to show your appreciation, why not drop the tip in the donation box?

The National Parks Conservation Association (NPCA) is just three years younger than the NPS itself – it was founded in 1919. It's another organization you can support to help preserve and improve the national park properties.

"... National Parks are the touchstones of our shared history and culture. In some ways, they represent the soul of the nation. They represent our hopes, our dreams, our struggles. They are our absolute best places,"

- Tom Kiernan, NPCA President.

The NPCA advocates for the National Park units and the National Park Service. It also educates "decision makers" and the public about the importance of preserving the parks and helps to convince members of Congress to uphold the existing laws that protect the parks and to support new legislation to address threats to the parks. Read about its work at *www.npca.org*.

"The most important thing I've learned from being involved with NPCA is that a single person can and does make a difference."

- NPCA Volunteer

The National Park Foundation, the fund-raising non-profit partner of the NPS, raises funds from private sources for partnership projects such as the Flight 93 National Memorial Campaign and the African American Experience. They help to fund the WebRangers program mentioned in Chapter 5 as well as the Parks' Electronic Field Trip program. They're at *http://www.nationalparks.org.*

Spreading the Word

When the National Park Service conducts nationwide visitor surveys, it receives consistently high ratings for many aspects of the units. In these surveys, one of the most interesting questions has been: "How did you hear about this park?" *Survey says:* The most common answer to that question is: "Word of mouth". People who visit NPS units tell their friends, parents, sisters, brothers-in-law, cousins, colleagues and neighbors about them, and that recommendation carries weight. You, too, can help spread the word by encouraging more people to discover and enjoy the treasures on their doorsteps. So there's something simple an individual can do to make a difference: if you enjoy a visit to an NPS unit, tell people about it – or take them there!

Political action

Throughout their history the status and preservation of National Park units seems to have been frequently threatened for one reason or another. Now in the twenty-first century public land is being eaten up for alternative energy projects, which encroach on wild habitat and crowd the borders of National Park sites. Mining and other interests wage constant battles to be allowed to develop wild areas. Federal budget fluctuations take their toll, too!

They're our parks, it's our government. We can make a difference. Take a look at your local legislators' voting records on park-related subjects and lobby them to support our parks. If you haven't done this before, maybe now's the time to try it! Encourage your legislators to support the National Parks; organize in your own community if necessary. Support, join and work with the National Parks Conservation Association, *npca.org,* the chief body coordinating political action to protect and enhance our National Parks.

∾

CHAPTER 8: What People Find in NPS Units

All sorts of people have different experiences and find different kinds of enjoyment, inspiration, comfort and peace in the National Park units. In this chapter some visitors and staff speak for themselves. These are all real comments from real people although I've changed names where people wished me to.

I wonder what *your* contribution to this chapter would be?

The Magic Forest

Evi, from Washington DC, finds that Great Falls, a part of the NPS unit known as the George Washington Memorial Parkway, is a place of natural beauty, a place to take visiting grandchildren and other family members, and a place to watch herons feeding and kayakers shooting the rapids like something out of a scary movie.

Great Falls is also an important part of her spiritual life: *"It's a wonderful refuge, and just knowing it's there offers that possibility. It's a balm to the soul – beautifully peaceful."*

Describing the walk down to the river, past the old C&O Canal, where costumed National Park rangers lead waterborne expeditions, she continued: *"It's the most wonderful place in the world. As you walk down to the river, it feels as if you're going into the magic forest.*

"I went during the Jewish New Year holiday as a spiritual practice to be near water, which is very important in the ritual of Yom Kippur. Great Falls is aesthetically wonderfully satisfying, and existentially it brings us in touch with forces that are larger than we are."

On the outskirts of a huge metropolitan area, Great Falls is still to be discovered by people like Evi's brother, who, having visited his sister in DC for many years, finally went there with her for the first time. His reaction was typical of those discovering these treasures on their doorsteps: *"Why have I never been here before?"*

How They Lived

Kavitaa, from Sedona, Arizona, has visited her local treasures Montezuma Castle National Monument and Tuzigoot National Monument many times:

"Visiting these sites over the years," she said, *"I've gained an understanding of how the Sinagua people lived here in the past, what it was like to live in this harsh climate, where it's so hot and dry a large part of the year.*

"I've learned how they used what is available here, the strands from yucca leaves for sandals, the walnuts and pine nuts for food and oils, the rocks to build their small rooms for sleeping and shelter.

"Sitting in the shade of large trees near water on a hot summer day, listening to birds and insects it seems they lived in a paradise, although one where often you had to be fit and able to climb ladders to get into your sleeping room for the night!"

A Portal to Empathy

For rangers, working daily in such evocative places, the connections become tangible:

"The porch at Franklin Roosevelt's Top Cottage in Hyde Park, New York, is unlike most porches. The cottage, tucked back in the woods, has hosted kings, queens, presidents, first

ladies, princesses, and prime ministers. On the porch was held the infamous picnic in 1939 when the King and Queen of England came to the United States looking for support in the months leading up to World War II and FDR treated them to their first experience of hotdogs!

"There's something about sitting on that porch that's hard to describe. The feeling of place is overwhelming. It was a place FDR designed to meet not only his personal interests, but also his physical needs. It was designed by a man in a wheelchair to use without assistance. It was a place where he was not afraid to show who he truly was, a man with physical limitations. To this day looking out on the view, listening to the birds, or watching the leaves falling in autumn, you get a sense of what it must have been like for FDR."

Ranger Kevin, Hyde Park, NY

A Final Vision

Hiking the Appalachian National Scenic Trail, Joan from Connecticut had a very sad encounter when she happened upon the body of hiker who had collapsed and died on the trail some time earlier.

"The doctors said he died instantly of heart failure," she said. *"He had fallen still holding his hiking sticks, his feet still on the trail. When I think back I can imagine the vision he had just experienced of the glorious view from the top of the hill then the*

open brightness of the trail leading downwards like a green tunnel. I hope that knowing he was enjoying a wonderful and peaceful place is some comfort to his family."

Amazingly Alone

Even the well-known NPS units can offer the unexpected, as Mary Ellen, from New Hampshire, found:

"What amazes me," she said, "is that we've had moments of just us: me and Sarah on the Fairyland Trail in Bryce Canyon, and me and Bill on the Taylor Creek Trail in Kolob Canyon at Zion, and just me early morning on North Kaibab Trail on the North Rim of the Grand Canyon. To be alone in the big parks is so amazing!"

A Speck in the Universe

Randy and Lisa, from East Barnard, Vermont, were traveling in California, somewhat overwhelmed by the sight of the many huge trees they drove past:

"Then we came to Muir Woods National Monument which is beautiful – it's down in a deep valley with these humungous trees growing right up" said Randy.

"When I stood inside a huge burned out tree I felt very, very small, like a speck in the Universe, just tiny," Lisa added, with a quiet smile that told of an awesome memory.

Named for a Pirate

Wendy, now living in Seattle, Washington, recalled her feelings about three very different National Park units:

"When I went to college in Ohio my friends always wanted to come back with me to my home in New Orleans. I learned about the city at Jean Lafitte National Historical Park and Preserve (JELA). It was named for a pirate who was a friend of the US.

"On ranger tours through the French Quarter I enjoyed learning about the different waves of immigration that created the country. Visiting JELA made a difference to how I felt about New Orleans – we moved a lot and the Park Service was how we got oriented to the place.

"I wonder what it looks like now."

She continued to remember other units: *"When I moved to Massachusetts in 1992 Lowell National Historical Park was recently established – I knew nothing about New England industry and I thought it was wonderful that Lowell interprets regular working class people – it was the first NPS site I'd seen doing that. It was also interesting to see how the opening of the park affected the local economy by creating jobs.*

"At Women's Rights National Historical Park, in Seneca NY, I was already aware of the event it commemorates: - the first ever women's rights convention, held in 1848. I was interested to

see that aspect of US history celebrated and surprised to see a
National Park that was mostly about dissent – about moments
in women's history and celebrating the other side of the story."

Clearing out the Pigeon Poop

Helping set up a new unit sometimes brings surprising challenges. Of Women's Rights NHP, Jan recalls: *"When the park
was being established a lot was known about the women involved
historically with women's rights, but not much was known about
the buildings in Seneca Falls! The building that's now a museum
had been a car dealership and pigeons had been living in the attic
for a long, long time, so the first thing we had to do was shovel out
the manure. We wore white clothing and respirators."*

Walking Among the Stars

Visitors from other parts of the world find enchantment
among these treasures, too. Here's the experience of Frances,
from Cardiff in the UK:

*"Camping one night at Abiquiu Lake, an Army Corps of
Engineers campsite in northern New Mexico, I met another trav-
eler. We sat around a campfire quietly exchanging stories until
I mentioned that the next day I planned to visit Chaco Culture
National Historical Park.*

*"His face, already illuminated by the flickering flames, bright-
ened further: "Ah," he said: "Chaco, the magic word!" He told*

me that he'd worked there for several years and studied the cosmology of this extraordinary place. I'd seen the movie "The Sun Dagger" that explains the astronomical observatory in Fajada Butte and the alignment of the now ruined buildings at Chaco, but this man had more to tell.

"He explained that the layout of the various buildings in the landscape reflects the constellations in a particular part of the sky: Orion, Sirius, and the Pleiades, because the people who built them came from beyond those stars. It was an enchanting cosmic image and the next day, following his directions, I walked the short pathway between two of the principal buildings, Pueblo Bonito and Chetro Ketl, with light in my heart, knowing that as I did so I was on a trail among the stars, walking along Orion's belt!"

Fajada Butte, Chaco Culture National Historical Park,
New Mexico

Being Prepared

Dan, from Geneseo, Illinois, reminds us of the value of prior research, or checking things out before we hit the road:

"I loved the Keys Ranch tour at Joshua Tree National Park. It was the highlight of our visit. You have to make reservations ahead of time, so if we hadn't asked about programs beforehand, if we'd just turned up at the park unprepared, we would never have known about it!"

On Your Doorstep

For Tom and Tonya in Woodstock, Vermont, living next door to Marsh-Billings-Rockefeller National Historical Park makes the 555-acre forest park their playground: *"We looked around a lot before we decided to buy a home, and this place has turned out to be the gem of our lives,"* said Tom.

Failure to capture

"I was aiming to hike right around Two Medicine Lake in Glacier National Park," Phyllis, from Massachusetts, remembered.

"Just as the trail emerged from the forest into a clearing, out popped a bear cub from the slope below. It was quickly joined by two siblings and I had three tubby cubs gathered on the trail ahead of me. By this time, I had my canister of bear spray unholstered ready for momma bear's appearance. She gave me a cursory glance and continued uphill, soon disappearing into

the brushy cover followed by the cubs. Frantically transitioning from bear spray to camera, a fuzzy photo of two cub butts was all I managed to shoot. However, that memorable hike will remain with me forever."

More Than a Road

Susan, from Boone, North Carolina, lives right beside the Blue Ridge Parkway. She said:

"I've always had some sort of relationship with the Parkway and now it's right on my doorstep. It makes a difference to me because it allows me to get away from my work. It's where I go to clear my head and calm myself down.

"The Parkway's so special – there are so many things I've done there. My parents used to take us to Mabry's Mill as kids to eat pancakes – my sister found a photo of me and my sixth grade friends there. And the Parkway is where I took my dog to get her used to hiking with me.

"I see it change through the seasons. I even find myself thinking: "My goodness, it's grown up since Thursday!" There's an old homestead I remember when it used to have a chimney, and one area looks sad in winter because there are a lot of very barren looking big dead trees: we call them Earth Dragons.

"I love the flowers; I might be feeling badly, then I see a rattlesnake plantain and I'll be so excited, like a little kid who's found a treasure.

"One reason the Parkway is special is because it's right here for me to get to – I feel like it's mine."

Susan, it *is* yours – it belongs to you and to all the other citizens of the USA, and it's quite literally a treasure on your doorstep!

∿

CHAPTER 9: The Past and Future of Our Treasures

There was a time when the idea of national parks didn't exist, just as there was a time when inventions like automobiles, personal computers or the Internet didn't exist, and someone had to come up with the concept. I find myself wondering why the people of the USA have managed to recognize and protect so many natural and cultural treasures.

Like most great ideas, the National Parks evolved out of social conditions, propelled by impulses such as an appreciation of nature and a wish to preserve open spaces for public recreation. They also grew from the commercial ambitions of railroad magnates and other entrepreneurs who planned to profit by bringing visitors from the populous East to view the wonders of the West. A culture of land ownership was another contributing factor: in earlier American societies, land ownership was different, with tribes using, rather than owning, certain territories, but once the European view of land ownership became widespread, the seeds were sown for the designation of some land as publically owned.

The large and diverse population of this country as well as widespread toleration for different cultures and perspectives, provide fertile ground for new ideas. It's possible here for individuals or small groups of people - or vested interests – to make a difference. And in a society where many people live above the subsistence level, there is time and leisure to devote to causes and activities other than finding food, water, shelter, and space for their families.

The Federal Government began setting aside special places as early as 1832 but the concept of a large park to be open to the public and federally maintained was not then current. The idea of setting aside land, removing it from industrial exploitation, was fueled by changing attitudes in society. The Romantic poets and painters of Europe infected the Americans with their admiration of the sublime in nature, and some Americans decided to preserve some land relatively undeveloped where people could enjoy such beauty.

Art reveals treasures of the Wests

George Catlin, an artist who explored the prairies and the Rockies in the 1830s, is usually attributed with the first use of the term "park" in the context of federal land. While painting an astounding collection of portraits of the people of nearly 50 different American Indian tribes, he noticed that their way of life was rapidly disappearing. In 1832 he suggested:

"a magnificent park, where the world could see for ages to come, the native Indian in his classic attire, galloping his wild horse, with sinewy bow, and shield and lance, amid the fleeting herds of elks and buffaloes. What a beautiful and thrilling specimen for America to preserve and hold up to the view of her refined citizens and the world, in future ages! A Nations Park, containing man and beast, in all the wild and freshness of their nature's beauty!"

I doubt that his idea of preserving the people along with the buffalo as "specimens" would find favor today! Nor did it take root in the 1830s and his suggestion was never acted upon. Whether Catlin's idea influenced later park makers is questionable, but he can at least claim to have used the term!

Catlin was just one of many painters and photographers who chronicled nineteenth century expeditions exploring the Rocky Mountains and the West, led by explorers and surveyors such as Frederick Lander. The artists' work influenced and excited public opinion and helped lead to federal designation of reserves and parks. Some of these painters, including Thomas Moran and Albert Bierstadt, are commemorated in the names of Rocky Mountain peaks, as is Lander himself. George Catlin was not honored in this way.

Also in 1832, part of the town of Hot Springs in Arkansas, an area of healing thermal waters well known to and used for many years by native people, was designated a Federal reservation. It came into the care of the Department of the Interior when that body was established in 1849 and was renamed "Hot Springs National Park" in 1921. Some people consider Hot Springs to have been the first national park, although it did not originally have that label.

Yosemite and Yellowstone

The idea of national parks simmered for some time: then in 1864 Congress protected the Yosemite Valley with an Act promoted by California senator John Conness and strongly supported by President Lincoln. The Valley, although federally designated, was given into the keeping of the State of California at that time. The well-known conservationist John Muir came into the picture a little later, discovered that the State was allowing the land to be exploited, and published several magazine articles that prompted the federal government to declare Yosemite a national park in 1890.

By this time Yellowstone, the unit that usually lays claim to being the first national park in the USA, had been set up in 1872, following the reports of expeditions in 1869-1871. Ferdinand Hayden led the 1871 expedition which included photographer William Henry Jackson and artists Henry W. Elliott and Thomas Moran, whose work caught the imagination of Congress when Hayden and others began promoting a park bill in Washington later that year.

Monumental legislation

The Antiquities Act of 1906, passed as an effort to curb the plundering of archaeological sites, is an important tool for creating NPS units. It legislated the establishment by Presidential decree of federally protected areas called National Monuments, thus providing a quicker and simpler route to protection than establishing a National Park, which requires an Act of Congress.

In 1906, President Theodore Roosevelt first used the Antiquities Act to protect Devil's Tower National Monument in Wyoming and, since then, more than 80 National Monuments have followed. Some iconic units such as Death Valley and the Grand Canyon were initially protected as National Monuments and later re-classified as National Parks. Retiring Presidents have sometimes used their powers under the Antiquities Act to establish a clutch of National Monuments in the last months of their term. Not all Monuments, however, have enjoyed universal acclaim and two states, Wyoming and Alaska, have found ways to limit the reach of the Antiquities Act.

Centennial

August 25, 1916, saw the creation of the National Park Service itself, a body which gathered together the eight then existing National Parks: Yellowstone; Yosemite; Sequoia; Mount Rainier; Crater Lake; Wind Cave; Mesa Verde; Glacier and Rocky Mountain, and around 17 existing National Monuments, under one administration with a specific mission which I'll restate here, using the 2016 wording:

"The National Park Service preserves unimpaired the natural and cultural resources and values of the National Park System for the enjoyment, education, and inspiration of this and future generations. The Park Service cooperates with partners to extend the benefits of natural and cultural resource conservation and outdoor recreation throughout this country and the world."

The Nation's Storyteller

More than 100 years ago, some people had enough vision and energy to set aside part of the relatively untouched land of North America – taken, of course, let us never forget, out of the hands and from beneath the feet of the native peoples.

To these wild lands have been added over the past century, through the advocacy of different individuals and organizations, many more areas of natural and cultural significance. Commercial and political interests have also played their part over the years. Whatever the motivation for their preservation, these places have great value: wild lands help balance the ever-increasing atmospheric carbon output of the human race; they provide havens for beleaguered plant and animal species, and their effect on the human soul is incalculable. We would be poorer for their loss, and for the loss of units that remind us of the prehistoric and historic development of this country and its culture.

We have reason to be grateful to all those who have had the foresight to set aside untouched forests, seashores, watersheds, and other wild areas, as well as historic sites and even areas that have been used and abused but can be reclaimed. I, for one, am grateful that we're able to protect our past, present and future, and the past, present and future of our children and grandchildren in this way.

The 400-plus National Park Service units embrace a vast range of habitats and preserve an endless treasure trove of stories. They rightly lay claim to the title of "The Nation's Storyteller". They elicit a huge variety of responses from the human psyche, heart, and soul. Somewhere among the 400 is one, or maybe several, sights and stories that will strike a chord with you, that will pique your interest, that will pull at your heartstrings, that will help your spirit soar.

Share and care

These places are ours to share and to care for. By participating, by visiting, by volunteering, by supporting and by spreading the word, we're doing something positive for ourselves, something that helps us learn, think, re-create, relax, exercise, enjoy, preserve, conserve and perhaps find new meaning in our lives by contemplating the meanings of these special places. We're also doing something important for our communities, our families, our children and grandchildren, our nation, and Planet Earth by appreciating, visiting, and caring for these special places.

There's a whole lot more to our National Park properties than mountains, canyons, lakes, bison and bears. And they may be closer to us than we think: right on our doorsteps. Please, in this centenary year, use, enjoy, and support all these places – we need to keep an eye on our treasures!

Happy 100th Birthday, National Park Service!

The End

National Park System Designations and Number of Units

As of February 2016
(Subject to change, especially since new National Monuments are often designated in the last few months of a presidential administration – watch this space!)

National Battlefields 11
National Battlefield Parks 4
National Battlefield Site 1
National Military Parks 9
National Historical Parks 50
National Historic Sites 78
International Historic Sites 1
National Lakeshores 4
National Memorials 30
National Monuments 81
National Parks 59
National Parkways 4
National Preserves 19
National Reserves 2
National Recreation Areas 18
National Rivers 5
National Wild and Scenic Rivers & Riverways 10
National Scenic Trails 3
National Seashores 10
Other Designations 11
Total Units 410

Find this list and an explanation of the various designations at *www.nps.gov* by searching for faqs

∾

APPENDIX 2:
National Park Units by State as of January 2016

Units spanning more than one state are listed only once. See *www.nps.gov* for more information about individual units.

Alabama	Horseshoe Bend National Military Park
	Little River Canyon National Preserve
	Russell Cave National Monument
	Tuskegee Airmen National Historic Site
	Tuskegee Institute National Historic Site
Alaska	Alagnak Wild River
	Aniakchak National Monument
	Aniakchak National Preserve
	Bering Land Bridge National Preserve
	Cape Krusenstern National Monument
	Denali National Park
	Denali National Preserve
	Gates of the Arctic National Park
	Gates of the Arctic National Preserve
	Glacier Bay National Park
	Glacier Bay National Preserve
	Katmai National Park

Katmai National Preserve

Kenai Fjords National Park

Klondike Gold Rush National Historical Park *(partially in WA)*

Kobuk Valley National Park

Lake Clark National Park

Lake Clark National Preserve

Noatak National Preserve

Sitka National Historical Park

World War II Valor in the Pacific National Monument *(partially in CA and HI)*

Wrangell-St. Elias National Park

Wrangell-St. Elias National Preserve

Yukon-Charley Rivers National Preserve

American Samoa | National Park of American Samoa

Arizona | Canyon De Chelly National Monument

Casa Grande Ruins National Monument

Chiricahua National Monument

Coronado National Memorial

Fort Bowie National Historic Site

Glen Canyon National Recreation Area *(partially in UT)*

Grand Canyon National Park

Hohokam Pima National Monument

Hubbell Trading Post National Historic Site

Montezuma Castle National Monument

Navajo National Monument

Organ Pipe Cactus National Monument

Petrified Forest National Park

Pipe Spring National Monument

Saguaro National Park

Sunset Crater Volcano National Monument

Tonto National Monument

Tumacacori National Historical Park

Tuzigoot National Monument

Walnut Canyon National Monument

Wupatki National Monument

Arkansas   Arkansas Post National Memorial

Buffalo National River

Little Rock Central High School National Historic Site

Fort Smith National Historic Site

Hot Springs National Park

Pea Ridge National Military Park

President William Jefferson Clinton Birthplace Home National Historic Site

California   Cabrillo National Monument

Castle Mountains National Monument

César E. Chávez National Monument

Channel Islands National Park

Death Valley National Park *(partially in NV)*

Devils Postpile National Monument

Eugene O'Neill National Historic Site

Fort Point National Historic Site

Golden Gate National Recreation Area

John Muir National Historic Site

Joshua Tree National Park

Kings Canyon National Park

Lassen Volcanic National Park

Lava Beds National Monument

	Manzanar National Historic Site
	Mojave National Preserve
	Muir Woods National Monument
	Pinnacles National Park
	Point Reyes National Seashore
	Port Chicago Naval Magazine National Memorial
	Redwood National Park
	Rosie the Riveter/World War II Home Front National Historical Park
	San Francisco Maritime National Historical Park
	Santa Monica Mountains National Recreation Area
	Sequoia National Park
	Whiskeytown-Shasta-Trinity National Recreation Area
	Yosemite National Park
Colorado	Bent's Old Fort National Historic Site
	Black Canyon of the Gunnison National Park
	Colorado National Monument
	Curecanti National Recreation Area
	Dinosaur National Monument *(partially in UT)*
	Florissant Fossil Beds National Monument
	Great Sand Dunes National Park
	Great Sand Dunes National Preserve
	Hovenweep National Monument *(partially in UT)*
	Mesa Verde National Park
	Rocky Mountain National Park

Sand Creek Massacre National Historic Site

Yucca House National Monument

Connecticut   Weir Farm National Historic Site

Delaware   First State National Historical Park *(partially in PA)*

Florida   Big Cypress National Preserve

Biscayne National Park

Canaveral National Seashore

Castillo de San Marcos National Monument

DeSoto National Memorial

Dry Tortugas National Park

Everglades National Park

Fort Caroline National Memorial

Fort Matanzas National Monument

Gulf Islands National Seashore *(partially in MS)*

Timucuan Ecological and Historic Preserve

Georgia   Andersonville National Historic Site

Chattahoochee River National Recreation Area

Chickamauga and Chattanooga National Military Park *(partially in TN)*

Cumberland Island National Seashore

Fort Frederica National Monument

Fort Pulaski National Monument

Jimmy Carter National Historic Site

Kennesaw Mountain National Battlefield Park

	Martin Luther King, Jr. National Historic Site
	Ocmulgee National Monument
Guam	War in the Pacific National Historical Park
Hawaii	Haleakala National Park
	Hawaii Volcanoes National Park
	Honouliuli National Monument
	Kalaupapa National Historical Park
	Kaloko-Honokohau National Historical Park
	Pu'uhonua O Honaunau National Historical Park
	Pu'ukohola Heiau National Historic Site
Idaho	City of Rocks National Reserve
	Craters of the Moon National Monument
	Craters of the Moon National Preserve
	Hagerman Fossil Beds National Monument
	Minidoka National Historic Site
	Nez Perce National Historical Park
Illinois	Lincoln Home National Historic Site
	Pullman National Monument
Indiana	George Rogers Clark National Historical Park
	Indiana Dunes National Lakeshore
	Lincoln Boyhood National Memorial
Iowa	Effigy Mounds National Monument
	Herbert Hoover National Historic Site
Kansas	Brown vs. Board of Education National Historic Site
	Fort Larned National Historic Site
	Fort Scott National Historic Site
	Nicodemus National Historic Site
	Tallgrass Prairie National Preserve

Kentucky	Abraham Lincoln Birthplace National Historical Park
	Cumberland Gap National Historical Park *(partially in TN and VA)*
	Mammoth Cave National Park
Louisiana	Cane River Creole National Historical Park
	Jean Lafitte National Historical Park and Preserve
	New Orleans Jazz National Historical Park
	Poverty Point National Monument
Maine	Acadia National Park
	Appalachian National Scenic Trail *(Maine to Georgia, 14 states)*
	Saint Croix Island International Historic Site
Maryland	Antietam National Battlefield
	Assateague Island National Seashore *(partially in VA)*
	Catoctin Mountain Park
	C & O Canal National Historical Park *(Partially in DC)*
	Clara Barton National Historic Site
	Fort McHenry National Monument and Historic Shrine
	Fort Washington Park
	Greenbelt Park
	Hampton National Historic Site
	Harriet Tubman Underground Railroad National Monument
	Monocacy National Battlefield

Piscataway Park

Potomac Heritage National Scenic Trail *(Partially in PA)*

Thomas Stone National Historic Site

Massachusetts   Adams National Historical Park

Blackstone River Valley National Historical Park *(Partially in RI)*

Boston African American National Historic Site

Boston Harbor Islands National Recreation Area

Boston National Historical Park

Cape Cod National Seashore

Frederick Law Olmstead National Historic Site

John F. Kennedy National Historic Site

Longfellow National Historic Site

Lowell National Historical Park

Minuteman National Historical Park

New Bedford Whaling National Historical Park

Salem Maritime National Historic Site

Saugus Iron Works National Historic Site

Springfield Armory National Historic Site

Michigan   Isle Royale National Park

Keweenaw National Historical Park

Pictured Rocks National Lakeshore

River Raisin National Battlefield Park

	Sleeping Bear Dunes National Lakeshore
Minnesota	Grand Portage National Monument
	Mississippi National River and Recreation Area
	Pipestone National Monument
	Voyageurs National Park
Mississippi	Brices Cross Roads National Battlefield Site
	Natchez National Historical Park
	Natchez Trace Parkway *(partially in AL, TN)*
	Natchez Trace National Scenic Trail *(partially in AL, TN)*
	Tupelo National Battlefield
	Vicksburg National Military Park *(partially in LA)*
Missouri	George Washington Carver National Monument
	Harry S Truman National Historic Site
	Jefferson National Expansion Memorial
	Ozark National Scenic Riverways
	Ulysses S. Grant National Historic Site
	Wilson's Creek National Battlefield
Montana	Big Hole National Battlefield
	Bighorn Canyon National Recreation Area
	Glacier National Park
	Grant-Kohrs Ranch National Historic Site
	Little Bighorn Battlefield National Monument
Nebraska	Agate Fossil Beds National Monument
	Homestead National Monument of America
	Missouri National Recreational River *(partially in SD)*

	Niobrara National Scenic River
	Scotts Bluff National Monument
Nevada	Great Basin National Park
	Lake Mead National Recreation Area *(partially in AZ)*
	Tule Springs Fossil Beds National Monument
New Hampshire	Saint-Gaudens National Historic Site
New Jersey	Great Egg Harbor Scenic and Recreational River
	Morristown National Historical Park
	Paterson Great Falls National Historical Park
	Thomas Edison National Historical Park
New Mexico	Aztec Ruins National Monument
	Bandelier National Monument
	Capulin Volcano National Monument
	Carlsbad Caverns National Park
	Chaco Culture National Historical Park
	El Malpais National Monument
	El Morro National Monument
	Fort Union National Monument
	Gila Cliff Dwellings National Monument
	Manhattan Project National Historical Park *(partially in TN and WA)*
	Pecos National Historical Park
	Petroglyph National Monument
	Salinas Pueblo Missions National Monument
	Valles Caldera National Preserve
	White Sands National Monument

New York	African Burial Ground National Monument
	Castle Clinton National Monument
	Eleanor Roosevelt National Historic Site
	Federal Hall National Memorial
	Fire Island National Seashore
	Fort Stanwix National Monument
	Gateway National Recreation Area *(partially in NJ)*
	General Grant National Memorial
	Governors Island National Monument
	Hamilton Grange National Memorial
	Home of Franklin D. Roosevelt National Historic Site
	Martin Van Buren National Historic Site
	Saint Paul's Church National Historic Site
	Sagamore Hill National Historic Site
	Saratoga National Historical Park
	Statue of Liberty National Monument *(partially in NJ)*
	Theodore Roosevelt Birthplace National Historic Site
	Theodore Roosevelt Inaugural National Historic Site
	Vanderbilt Mansion National Historic Site
	Women's Rights National Historical Park
North Carolina	Blue Ridge Parkway *(partially in VA)*
	Cape Hatteras National Seashore
	Cape Lookout National Seashore

Carl Sandburg Home National Historic Site

Fort Raleigh National Historic Site

Guilford Courthouse National Military Park

Moores Creek National Battlefield

Wright Brothers National Memorial

North Dakota   Fort Union Trading Post National Historic Site *(partially in MT)*

Knife River Indian Villages National Historic Site

Theodore Roosevelt National Park

Ohio   Charles Young Buffalo Soldiers National Monument

Cuyahoga Valley National Park

Dayton Aviation Heritage National Historical Park

First Ladies National Historic Site

Hopewell Culture National Historical Park

James A. Garfield National Historic Site

Perry's Victory and International Peace Memorial

William Howard Taft National Historic Site

Oklahoma   Chickasaw National Recreation Area

Washita Battlefield National Historic Site

Oregon   Crater Lake National Park

Lewis and Clark National Historical Park *(partially in WA)*

John Day Fossil Beds National Monument

Oregon Caves National Monument and Preserve

Pennsylvania	Allegheny Portage Railroad National Historic Site
	Delaware Water Gap National Recreation Area *(partially in NJ)*
	Edgar Allan Poe National Historic Site
	Eisenhower National Historic Site
	Flight 93 National Memorial
	Fort Necessity National Battlefield
	Friendship Hill National Historic Site
	Gettysburg National Military Park
	Hopewell Furnace National Historic Site
	Independence National Historical Park
	Johnstown Flood National Memorial
	Middle Delaware National Scenic River
	Steamtown National Historic Site
	Thaddeus Kosciuszko National Memorial
	Upper Delaware Scenic and Recreational River *(partially in NY)*
	Valley Forge National Historical Park
Puerto Rico	San Juan National Historic Site
Rhode Island	Roger Williams National Memorial
South Carolina	Charles Pinckney National Historic Site
	Congaree National Park
	Cowpens National Battlefield
	Fort Sumter National Monument
	Kings Mountain National Military Park
	Ninety Six National Historic Site
South Dakota	Badlands National Park
	Jewel Cave National Monument
	Minuteman Missile National Historic Site

	Mount Rushmore National Memorial
	Wind Cave National Park
Tennessee	Andrew Johnson National Historic Site
	Big South Fork National River and Recreation Area *(partially in KY)*
	Fort Donelson National Battlefield *(partially in KY)*
	Great Smoky Mountains National Park *(partially in NC)*
	Obed Wild and Scenic River
	Shiloh National Military Park *(partially in MS)*
	Stones River National Battlefield
Texas	Alibates Flint Quarries National Monument
	Amistad National Recreation Area
	Big Bend National Park
	Big Thicket National Preserve
	Chamizal National Memorial
	Fort Davis National Historic Site
	Guadalupe Mountains National Park
	Lake Meredith National Recreation Area
	Lyndon B. Johnson National Historical Park
	Padre Island National Seashore
	Palo Alto Battlefield National Historical Park
	Rio Grande Wild and Scenic River
	San Antonio Missions National Historical Park
	Waco Mammoth National Monument
Utah	Arches National Park
	Bryce Canyon National Park
	Canyonlands National Park

	Capitol Reef National Park
	Cedar Breaks National Monument
	Golden Spike National Historic Site
	Natural Bridges National Monument
	Rainbow Bridge National Monument
	Timpanogos Cave National Monument
	Zion National Park
Vermont	Marsh-Billings-Rockefeller National Historical Park
Virgin Islands	Buck Island Reef National Monument
	Christiansted National Historic Site
	Salt River Bay National Historical Park and Ecological Preserve
	Virgin Islands National Park
	Virgin Islands Coral Reef National Monument
Virginia	Appomattox Court House National Historical Park
	Arlington House, The Robert E. Lee Memorial
	Booker T. Washington National Monument
	Cedar Creek and Belle Grove National Historical Park
	Colonial National Historical Park
	Fort Monroe National Monument
	Fredericksburg and Spotsylvania National Military Park
	George Washington Birthplace National Monument
	George Washington Memorial Parkway *(partially in MD, DC)*
	Maggie L. Walker National Historic Site

	Manassas National Battlefield Park
	Petersburg National Battlefield Park
	Prince William Forest Park
	Richmond National Battlefield Park
	Shenandoah National Park
	Wolf Trap National Park for the Performing Arts
Washington	Ebey's Landing National Historical Reserve
	Fort Vancouver National Historic Site *(partially in OR)*
	Lake Chelan National Recreation Area
	Lake Roosevelt National Recreation Area
	Mount Rainier National Park
	North Cascades National Park
	Olympic National Park
	Ross Lake National Recreation Area
	San Juan Island National Historical Park
	Whitman Mission National Historic Site
Washington DC	Carter G. Woodson Home National Historic Site
	Constitution Gardens
	Ford's Theatre National Historic Site
	Franklin D. Roosevelt Memorial
	Frederick Douglass National Historic Site
	Korean War Veterans Memorial
	Lincoln Memorial
	Lyndon Baines Johnson Memorial Grove on the Potomac
	Martin Luther King, Jr. Memorial
	Mary McLeod Bethune Council House National Historic Site

	National Capital Parks
	National Mall
	Pennsylvania Avenue National Historic Site
	Rock Creek Park
	Theodore Roosevelt Island
	Thomas Jefferson Memorial
	Vietnam Veterans Memorial
	Washington Monument
	White House
	World War I Memorial
	World War II Memorial
West Virginia	Bluestone National Scenic River
	Gauley River National Recreation Area
	Harpers Ferry National Historical Park *(partially in MD, VA)*
	New River Gorge National River
Wisconsin	Apostle Islands National Lakeshore
	Saint Croix National Scenic Riverway
Wyoming	Devils Tower National Monument
	Fort Laramie National Historic Site
	Fossil Butte National Monument
	Grand Teton National Park
	John D. Rockefeller Memorial Parkway
	Yellowstone National Park *(partially in ID, MT)*

Note from the author:

Thank you for joining me on this journey through the idea of what our National Park units are and what they can mean to us. Please enjoy them, and let me know about your adventures by emailing toyd@together.net or by posting a comment on the Treasures On Your Doorstep blog at:

http://treasuresonyourdoorstep.blogspot.com/.

About the author:

A few years ago, Welsh storyteller Julia Lynam found herself quite unexpectedly donning a ranger hat and discovering the kaleidoscopic world of the National Park units of the USA. "Treasures On Your Doorstep" is her way of sharing her discoveries with you. It's a mine of information and insights that will unlock hidden treasures for you all over the country.

Julia's home base is in Vermont, but she's never quite sure where her next job will take her.

Illustrators:

Melanie Gillman, who drew most of the interior illustrations, is an alumna of the Center for Cartoon Studies in White River Junction, Vermont. Melanie.Gillman@Colorado.edu

Jessica Valin, a mom, school nurse, organic gardener and artist, drew the young black bear in Chapter 6.

Acknowledgements

Thank you to friends, colleagues and family members who helped with the development of this work in their many different ways, including: Paula Barstow; Tereska Buko; Sybil Carey; Cindy Carss; Vesna Dye; Sonja Hakala; Laurie Huse; Tori Marshall; Karen Michaud; Eileen and John Myers; Jamie Richards; Stephen Scott; Joanne Shapp; Jessica and Marc Valin; and all the wonderful friends, acquaintances and complete strangers who are quoted in these pages. Some details have been changed to protect people's privacy!

Treasures On Your Doorstep
is a great gift idea
for friends and family.

To order more copies please go to:
www.createspace.com\3861485
or
www.Treasuresonyourdoorstep.com

This book is also available through Amazon.com and other retailers

Kindle version
Treasures On Your Doorstep is available as a Kindle e-book

Blog
Find the Treasures On Your Doorstep blog at:
http://treasuresonyourdoorstep.blogspot.com/

Wholesale
Please email toyd@together.net

ISBN: 978-0-9847805-1-8

www.ingramcontent.com/pod-product-compliance
Lightning Source LLC
Chambersburg PA
CBHW071002040426
42443CB00007B/617